NORWEGIAN SWEATER TECHNIQUES
for Today's Knitter

THERESE CHYNOWETH

Wiley Publishing, Inc.

Norwegian Sweater Techniques for Today's Knitter

Copyright © 2010 by Wiley Publishing, Inc., Hoboken, New Jersey. All rights reserved.

Published by Wiley Publishing, Inc., Hoboken, New Jersey

For general information on our other products and services or to obtain technical support please contact our Customer Care Department within the U.S. at (877) 762-2974, outside the U.S. at (317) 572-3993 or fax (317) 572-4002.

Wiley also publishes its books in a variety of electronic formats. Some content that appears in print may not be available in electronic books. For more information about Wiley products, please visit our web site at www.wiley.com.

Library of Congress Cataloging-in-Publication Data:

Chynoweth, Therese, 1958–
 Norwegian sweater techniques for today's knitter / by Therese Chynoweth.
  p. cm.
 ISBN-13: 978-0-470-48455-5
 ISBN-10: 0-470-48455-1
 1. Knitting--Patterns. 2. Knitting--Norway. 3. Sweaters--Norway. I. Title.
 TT825.C424 2010
 746.43'2041—dc22
                2010002933

Printed in China

10 9 8 7 6 5 4 3 2 1

Book production by Wiley Publishing, Inc., Composition Services

CREDITS

Acquisitions Editor
ROXANE CERDA

Project Editor
DONNA WRIGHT

Editorial Manager
CHRISTINA STAMBAUGH

Publisher
CINDY KITCHEL

Vice President and Executive Publisher
KATHY NEBENHAUS

Interior Design
ELIZABETH BROOKS

Cover Design
JOSÉ ALMAGEUR

Photography
BRIEN RICHMOND

Fabric swatch photo
©iStockphoto.com/tomograf

Norwegian seascape photo
©iStockphoto.com/uniseller

ACKNOWLEDGMENTS

The first person I should thank is my agent, Linda Roghaar. Without your persistence, this book would probably have never happened. To Roxane Cerda and Donna Wright at Wiley for holding my hand and helping me through my first book. To Rita Greenfeder, my technical editor, for helping me look good. To the ladies who helped with knitting the pieces for this book, Debbie Thayer, Lucinda Heller, Nancy Vogt, Pat Geiger, and Sandy Hybinette. Without you, I'd probably still be knitting. Special thanks to Dale of Norway, Inc. for permission to use three old designs in this book; each of these patterns is identified as a Dale Design in Part IV. And thanks to Singer/Viking Husqvarna for providing the sewing machine used in the photos.

I also need to thank my sisters, Margo and Gwen, and my mother, Margaret, for their enthusiasm and moral support, as well as tolerating my answer of "knitting" whenever they asked what I was doing. To friends back in Wisconsin, Beth Herbert, Gayle Mitterer, Heidi Rettler, Helen Stewart, Karren Fabian, and Laura Powers for their moral support during a stressful time. To Bea Ellis, Mary Ann Stephens, and Nancy Thorvilson for the suggestions and answers to a variety of questions.

Lastly, I'd like to thank Betsy Welch for encouraging me to submit designs to the knitting magazines, as well as Henrik Lumholdt and Olav Muench for having allowed me to play with yarn at work.

This book is for my mother, Margaret, and late father, Robert.
You always encouraged us to do what we loved,
and have always been there for us.

NORWEGIAN SWEATER TECHNIQUES

TABLE OF CONTENTS

IV PATTERNS

Introduction

My favorite knitting books are those that combine inspirational patterns with extensive technique instruction. As a knitter who is mostly self-taught, I find it terribly frustrating to open a book or magazine only to discover that the special techniques used in creating the design are described in a single, short paragraph, making it difficult to teach myself the technique. I've found that most books available on Norwegian knitting, although they showcase beautiful designs, contain very little in the way of practical how-to for the actual garment finishing. Out of that frustration, the idea for this book was born.

My goals here are to present in one place, as clearly as possible, the necessary steps to complete a sweater using Norwegian finishing techniques and take the fear out of cutting into hand-knit fabric. Since I'm a very visual person, I wanted to include plenty of illustrations and thorough descriptions of each of the steps involved, with a focus on those techniques not covered extensively in other books on Norwegian knitting. The patterns in this book demonstrate how these techniques can be used with any fiber and for much more than just knitting ski sweaters.

There are numerous references to, and comparisons with, Fair Isle knitting techniques. Many knitters may be familiar with Fair Isle knitting but not necessarily with Norwegian knitting and will tend to assume that because they're similar in appearance, they're also worked in the same way. Even though there are similarities between the two knitting traditions, there are differences that can be confusing at first, especially when it comes to the use of steeks or, as they're known in Norwegian knitting, cutting stitches. Once you've learned the Norwegian knitting and finishing techniques in this book, it'll be easy to develop your personal hybrid of techniques, blending both traditions.

The material presented here is organized in much the same way that I present it when teaching workshops: Part I gives an overview of the subject; Part II explores the steps involved in knitting the garment; Part III dives into the finishing, namely the sewing and cutting, which is usually seen as the scary part and often least discussed; and finally, Part IV contains the patterns.

Inspiration for the designs in this book came mainly from the yarns I used. Selecting the yarns for the patterns was surprisingly difficult given the wealth of fibers and yarn types available. I prefer to use natural fibers in much of my own personal knitting but had a lot of fun exploring other options. Machine stitching before cutting opens an entire new world of possibilities in yarn choices and projects.

I invite you to explore the world of Norwegian finishing techniques. Use this book to inspire your knitting as it has mine. There's no longer any need to be afraid to cut into your knitting, so go forth and cut without fear!

PART I
EXPLORING NORWEGIAN CONSTRUCTION TECHNIQUES

CHAPTER 1

Why Knit in the Round?

At first glance, knitting in the round (also known as circular knitting) may seem frightening or too difficult, but on closer examination, you'll find many advantages to working in the round. It's almost as old as knitting itself, whose origins are a mystery, and has been used wherever knitting has been practiced. Circular knitting gained a very undeserved reputation as "peasant" knitting in the mid-nineteenth century when flat patterns for the latest fashions were becoming available through new needle arts publications that focused on the emerging middle-class woman with free time on her hands. The idea that circular knitting was something only the lower classes did to earn a living through production knitting lasted well into the twentieth century.

Over the past few decades, circular knitting has been regaining some of its popularity (although there have still been many patterns written during this time that call for knitting pieces flat). The explosion in the popularity of Fair Isle designs during the late 1980s and '90s exposed many knitters to the idea of not only working in the round, but to *stranded* (or Fair Isle) knitting as well. New generations of knitters were reintroduced to the idea of working the body as one piece. Even so, many patterns currently appearing in books, magazines, and on the Internet are still worked flat and seamed, despite the fact that it would be very easy to convert these patterns to circular knitting. Yet most patterns worked in the round are rated as intermediate or even advanced.

One of my favorite features of knitting in the round is no side or underarm seams (and two fewer ends to be woven in for each eliminated seam). Finishing has never been one of my favorite parts of knitting, so any time I can get away with not having to sew another seam or weave in ends, I'm happy. Many garment patterns that are written to be worked flat, at the most basic level, consist of two rectangles and two trapezoids. Finishing has always felt like an afterthought and, I believe, is a good reason why some knitters never do their own finishing. The Norwegian methods covered in this book incorporate garment finishing into the entire construction process.

Because both front and back are worked at the same time, the tension is the same for both pieces—who hasn't spent many hours making a separate back and front only to find that their tension wasn't consistent and one piece is longer and wider than the other? This is also one reason some knitters work both sleeves, whether flat or in the round, at the same time.

Differences in tension between knit rows and purl rows is another reason why working in the round is a great idea. The vast majority of knitters don't purl at the same tension as they knit (did you ever notice horizontal stripes in your stockinette?), or at the same speed. Working in the round will give you a more evenly tensioned result, and if speed is important, it will also work up more quickly.

A number of knitters don't like to purl; some do what has been referred to as *knitting back backward* in order to avoid having to turn their work and purl across the wrong side. Have they ever realized they're actually knitting every alternate row left-handed? This could cause its own problems with uneven tension.

For the most part, working in the round eliminates the need of having to purl, except for texture patterns, ribbing, or when working back and forth after dividing for armholes or neck openings. Using steeks even eliminates the need to do that! For anyone unfamiliar with Fair Isle knitting, *steek* is a term used when referring to the stitches that are added for openings and later cut so that knitting continues in the round. Norwegian knitting tradition doesn't have a special name for these stitches and usually just refers to cutting stitches. More on this later!

A distinct advantage to working in the round has to be that you will always see your pattern on the right side as you knit. Anyone who has tried to purl a stranded pattern from the wrong side can attest to how confusing it can be.

Almost all pattern stitches can be worked in the round, with the exception of a few lace-type stitches and intarsia. (Although there is a limited amount of intarsia that can be worked in the round, too, it's still one technique that is best worked flat.) Cables, when worked back and forth, need an odd number of rows between crossings so that they can always be crossed on the right side of the work. When knitting in the round, you don't need to follow that rule and can cross a cable on any round you like.

Anyone concerned about garment shaping such as darts, waists, armholes, and necklines can rest assured that most shaping can be done in the round, too. About the only shaping that needs to be worked back and forth is when binding off multiple stitches at one time to shape the lower portion of an armhole or crewneck opening. In that case, you can work a few rows back and forth, then cast on stitches for a steek, and continue in the round. Alternately, shaping can be done by decreasing a single stitch each round to shape the opening. The former method will allow you to give your garment a more fashionable silhouette, while the latter will have a more traditional look.

Finally, for the knitter who desires a garment made in a more traditional manner, knitting in the round is the way to go. Just as there is no single *right* way to do anything in knitting, there are an unlimited number of techniques, from folk to fashion, that can be incorporated into your work. Let all of them inspire you!

CHAPTER 2

The Role of Steeks

Knitters who also sew will readily appreciate the role that steeks can play in knitting and the fact that you're actually creating fabric while knitting. For anyone who doesn't sew, the concept of cutting into your work can be very foreign, and something to be avoided wherever possible. The usual reaction is, "What do you mean I have to cut?" I struggled less with the idea of cutting into my first Fair Isle project than with cutting fabric that I'd hand-woven.

I've taught numerous workshops over the past 10 years where students came into the class and were terrified with the idea of cutting into their work. After the class, though, they laughed at how easy it was to do. When properly prepared, those stitches won't be going anywhere. Be prepared to want to cut everything.

I've already referred to steeks in the previous chapter, but I haven't yet defined them. *Steeks* are special cutting stitches that give you a seam allowance with which to work once the piece is sliced open and are most commonly found in Fair Isle stranded colorwork patterns. Steek is used rather loosely today by many knitters to refer to any stitches that are cut in order to create a cardigan front, armhole, or any other opening that wasn't knit into the work.

Fair Isle knitting patterns commonly refer to steeks, usually 10 extra stitches cast on at the beginning for a cardigan front, or added once armhole stitches are bound off or slipped to a holder. These steeks are worked with the first and last stitch always in the background color, and the stitches between worked in a *seeding* pattern—alternating single stitches of each color every round so that the whole effect is that of a tiny checkerboard. An alternate method is to work the colors in vertical stripes. Once the opening has been cut, excess width is trimmed away, leaving two or three stitches on each half of the opening.

Cut front edge of a cardigan.

Norwegian knitting patterns vary on the use of cutting stitches, and no special name is given to them. Depending on the knitting gauge, location, and width of the desired opening, there can be as few as three cutting stitches or as many as five more. If the extra stitches were added with the original number cast on, or added above a bound-off hole, these stitches are normally worked in just the background color throughout, either in stockinette (with the knit side showing) or in reverse stockinette (with the purl side showing). In cases where no extra stitches were added, such as armholes of drop shoulder sweaters, the pattern is typically continued across the area that will be cut.

For all the fear that the idea of cutting into a piece of knitting conjures for many knitters, the technique is really quite simple and elegant. Coarse wools easily lend themselves to the Fair Isle method, where the steeks are not normally stitched along the outer stitches; the coarseness of the wool helps to keep the strands in place, and the wool will felt with repeated wearing and washing. Smoother wools and other fibers, especially slippery cottons, silks, and other fibers lacking the scales found on wool, need help staying together. Here is where the Norwegian method really stands out!

Machine stitching is the preferred method of preparing any opening for cutting in the Norwegian method; although the loose ends may fray after cutting, the machine stitching helps to lock the strands of yarn in place so they can be cut without pulling apart. This works on wool, cotton, silk, linen, rayon, and bamboo, as well as other fibers and blends. This versatile technique is not just for ski sweaters! All of the designs in this book were sewn and cut in one way or another.

Uses for steeks and cut openings range from the usual armholes, to cardigan and vest fronts, to shaping necklines, to zipper openings. Add a zipper to a pullover, or convert a pullover to a cardigan, or a pullover vest to a vest with buttons or a zipper. Whether you choose to knit a plain piece or one with color-stranded patterns, steeks are versatile and can be combined with other techniques in any number of ways; the only limit is your imagination.

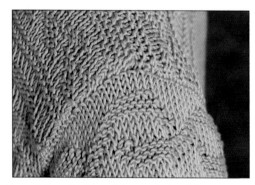

Steeks, or cutting stitches, were used at the neck of the Bonsai Shawl (left) and the armhole of the Cruise Pullover (right).

CHAPTER 3

How Facings Fit into the Picture

One of the features I like about the Norwegian finishing method is that facings are used to cover cut edges. Wherever a cut edge has been created, there's a facing that is either worked while the main piece is being knit, or added after the cutting has been done. The beauty of the facing is that it covers the cut edge, thus protecting it from wear and tear. Your garment will have a neater finish on the inside, similar in look to a couture finish.

Facings can be worked in a number of different ways. The easiest method is to just work extra length or width onto a piece and fold the extra portion over a cut edge, as is the case with sleeves for drop shoulder sweaters, or a cardigan front band that has been worked vertically.

Another option—one that is perfect for shaped edges or ribbed bands worked horizontally from stitches picked up along the cut edge—is to pick up stitches along the cut edge after the sleeve or band is sewn in and then work a few rows of stockinette. After binding off, fold the facing over the cut edge and sew it to the wrong side. If you're working with a heavier yarn, use a lighter-weight yarn for the facing to reduce bulk at that edge. For ribbed button/buttonhole band fronts, this eliminates a lot of bulk right at the band by spreading some of it away from the center.

Inside of armhole on the Green Line Pullover showing facing.

Wrong side of front band on the Royal Llama Linen Cardigan.

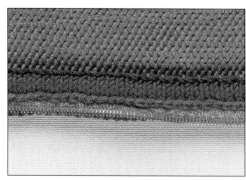

Wrong side of front band on the Zara Cardigan.

A variation on the knit facing is to use ribbon or braid to cover the cut edge. These facings can be placed on the right, or public, side of the garment to become a decorative element. Even when used on the wrong side, a decorative ribbon will add a nice touch to the front edge of a cardigan or pullover with a split neck.

Finally, adding facings as you do the finishing takes some of the *afterthought* feeling out of completing the sweater. There's still ample opportunity to add your own touches to the finishing, making the item that much more an expression of your creativity!

Ribbon around armhole on the Daylily Cardigan.

Use of the facing on the right side on the Blue Sky Wrap.

CHAPTER 4

Neckline Variations

The neckline is probably one of the most visible parts of any garment because it frames the wearer's face and neck. A well-designed and well-executed neckline is important to how the garment is perceived—is it well proportioned? Does it suit the piece? And most importantly, if the garment is a pullover, will it fit over the wearer's head?

Knowing how to work several styles of necklines is a great tool for any knitter to have at their disposal. As with armholes, there are always several variations that can be used.

CREWNECKS

Crownecks are probably one of the most familiar neck shapes and can be used on a wide variety of clothing styles. The first and most traditional method by which these necklines are made in Norway is to knit the entire garment in the round to the shoulder and then bind off; if you've ever knit a boatneck pullover, this is the sort of neck used. However, unlike the boatneck, the crewneck worked in this way will need to be marked for the neck width and depth on both the front and back of the body. The shape of the neck opening is machine stitched and the excess cut away. Take care, though, when marking and stitching the neckline to keep the shape symmetrical on each side, and not distort the piece while stitching.

The second method to create a crewneck line is to bind off stitches at the center front to begin the opening and then continue to the end of the round at the left side of the body. This leaves you with an opening about one-quarter of the way across the round for your front-neck opening. At that point, you'll need to begin working back and forth over the remainder of the body.

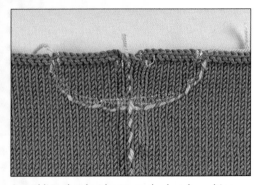

A neckline that has been marked and machine stitched, and is ready to cut.

When dealing with a colorwork or stitch pattern, it's very important to shift the beginning of the rows from the left side to the front neck edges. If you neglect to shift the beginning of the row, you'll end up with the same row being worked twice over the left shoulder.

Shaping the back neck opening is done much the same way, though after the initial bind-off to begin the back neck, each side of the body (both front and back of each shoulder) is worked separately.

A third method that can be used for crewnecks is to do the initial bind-off for the front neck edge and then cast on a steek so that work can continue in the round. The advantage of using this method is that you can continue working the color pattern in the round from the right side. One disadvantage to this method is that neck shaping is limited to single stitch decreases, limiting the amount of curve given to the neck edge; the previous method of working back and forth is ideal for a more curved shape.

The fourth method is a hybrid of the second and third methods and involves working the first few rows of neck shaping back and forth so that multiple stitches can be bound off at the beginning of several rows (typically four to eight for a curved neck shape). Once the neck shaping has reached a point of decreasing one stitch on each side, add a steek so work can continue in the round.

SQUARE NECKLINES

Square necklines can be made in any of the crewneck methods but without additional shaping after the initial bind-off of stitches. The second and third methods—which involve working back and forth after the initial bind-off and the steeked version—will be used more frequently in square neckline patterns, such as the Falk Cardigan on page 72.

V-NECKLINES

V-necklines can be worked using the crewneck methods as well. However, if the sweater has a great deal of color pattern to be worked across the upper body, I recommend adding a steek so that you can continue in the round to the shoulders. One thing to be aware of when using a steek for a V-neck is that the additional shaping on each side of the steek will result in very narrow (and extremely odd-looking) shoulders, and an equally small-looking neck opening. This, of course, will be solved once you've machine-stitched and cut open the neckline, but it may prove a little tricky to do the sewing on smaller garments.

Square neck with a steek.

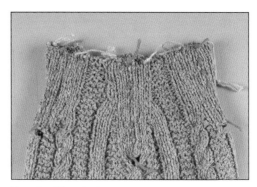

V-neck with a steek.

CHAPTER 5

Pick Your Sleeves

S leeves for traditional Norwegian sweaters vary from drop shoulder style to shaped with sleeve caps. As with Fair Isle sweaters, the sleeves of early Norwegian sweaters were picked up around the armhole and then worked down to the cuff. Modern Norwegian designs call for sleeves that are worked from the cuff up and then sewn in after cutting open the armhole.

The basic sleeve for most Norwegian sweaters fits a body with either drop shoulders or square armholes. In a drop-shoulder application, the armholes are fairly deep and sleeves are straight across the top, without a sleeve cap. Sleeves for a sweater with square armholes have minimal or no shaping at the top edge, and armholes are still fairly deep. Once the required underarm length is reached, the sleeve cap is made by continuing to work the pattern back and forth rather than in the round. For both basic sleeve types, the facing is commonly added at the top edge once the finished sleeve length is reached and before binding off. Normally worked with the background color or last pattern color used, these facings are done in reverse stockinette (the purl side showing while knitting, but the knit side showing on the inside of the body once the sleeve is sewn in). Other options to the facing knit at the top of the sleeve (such as ribbon or braid) were mentioned in chapter 3.

Top of sleeve for a drop shoulder sweater.

Top of sleeve for a square armhole.

When a garment has a shaped armhole and sleeve cap, the armhole often has a somewhat closer fit, yet will usually still accommodate a shirt underneath without binding at the underarm. If a steek has been added to the body once the initial armhole bind-off has been done, the facing will be made after the sleeve is sewn into the armhole.

For an armhole where the body was divided into separate front and back sections following the initial underarm bind-off, there is no need for a facing around that armhole and the sleeve is sewn in place as usual.

Shaped armhole with facing stitches being worked.

CHAPTER 6

Shoulder Finishes

Many knitters have a favorite method for joining shoulders and use it for every sweater they make. Hiding the shoulder seam is the goal.

Not only does the shoulder join (at its most obvious) connect the front and back edges, but the seam also needs to support both the weight of the body and the weight of the sleeves without stretching. Some forms of joining shoulders succeed better than others. One particularly popular method—grafting, or Kitchener stitch—works well for sleeveless and short-sleeve garments, or with very lightweight yarns, but should not be used for heavier yarns and long sleeves.

The three-needle bind-off is a wonderfully simple and functional shoulder join, and is most commonly worked so that the bound-off edges are on the inside. When worked so the bound-off edges are on the right side, it forms a visible ridge; this is a commonly used Norwegian shoulder join.

Two unique methods of two-needle bind-off have been used in Norway. Both of these bind-offs result in very functional and stable seams and are well suited for most types of garments.

The first form of two-needle bind-off begins by slipping both sets of shoulder stitches to the same needle, alternating a stitch from the front, and then a stitch from the back. Working the joining row is a bit trickier than the three-needle bind-off, but the look of the finished edge is similar.

A second two-needle Norwegian method is worked with live stitches on both needles, and alternates between purling two stitches together on the left needle and then

Shoulder of the Daylily Cardigan (above) and Cotton Jeans Henley (below) were both joined using the second two-needle method.

purling two stitches together on the right needle. The look on the right side is similar to that of a grafted seam but is much more stable. On the wrong side, however, there are two parallel lines of stitches that run perpendicular to the direction of the main work. A variation can be worked by knitting the joining row instead of purling it; in this case, the line of stitches running perpendicular to the main work will be on the right side.

Right side view of shoulder of the Zara Cardigan.

Inside view of shoulder of the Zara Cardigan.

A final method of joining shoulders, or any other bound-off edges, is to work one row of reverse stockinette before binding off. The seam is made by sewing both bound-off edges together using whipstitch in matching yarn color but worked from the outside. This creates a decorative effect at the shoulder, and the resulting seam lies flat on the inside and is wonderfully stable.

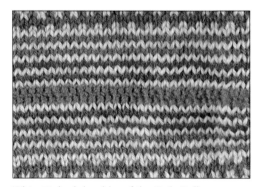

Whipstitched shoulder of the Heilo Pullover.

PART II
ANATOMY OF A SWEATER

CHAPTER 7

Reading Norwegian Charts

Multiple colors and intricate designs are very characteristic of the patterns most often associated with Norwegian sweater designs. Stranded knitting and chart reading are important skills to know when working any traditional Norwegian designs. Although these skills will take some practice to feel comfortable with while working, they are easy to learn.

If you are acquainted with Fair Isle knitting, handling two colors for stranded knitting will already be familiar to you. Norwegian knitting charts, on the other hand, are frequently different from Fair Isle charts and can be confusing if you're not aware of differences between the two pattern traditions. The most common error is to read a Norwegian color chart as if it were a Fair Isle chart, where the design repeats very nicely around the body and finishes with a complete repeat at the end of the round.

Norwegian colorwork patterns typically fall into one of three categories: a basic pattern based on a simple repeat and worked across the round much the same as a Fair Isle pattern; a nonrepeating pattern with a central motif that forms a mirror image at the center of both the front and back, and begins and ends at the sides of the body; and an allover pattern, usually with a motif centered on the back, that is worked over most of the back and front with a smaller pattern placed on each side of the front. A description of each type of pattern follows, along with sample charts.

NOTE

Here are some helpful hints if you are having trouble keeping the pattern correct on each round: In addition to the beginning of round markers and side markers, place different color markers at the end of every repeat or every other repeat (depending on the size of each repeat and what you feel comfortable with). When working each round, as you reach each marker you should be at the end of a repeat; if not, you'll only have a few stitches to rip back instead of an entire round. And for complex, nonrepeating patterns, it can be helpful to string small, lettered beads onto small pieces of yarn and slip these onto your needle every 10 stitches or so, and mark the chart to correspond to the letters. This will make finding your place in the chart much easier if you need to stop frequently.

BASIC PATTERNS

In Fair Isle knitting, it's very easy to tell if the pattern repeat will fit the piece because the repeat is evenly divisible into the total number of stitches on the needles. For instance, if the pattern repeat is 18 stitches wide and the body is 252 stitches, the repeat will be worked 14 times across each round—7 times on the front and 7 times on the back. Each additional size is usually reduced or enlarged by four repeats, maintaining the same number of pattern repeats on both the front and back, and keeping the same pattern stitch at the center of the front and back for each size. As an example, the pattern may call for 10 repeats worked on the smallest size, 14 repeats on the next size, and then 18 repeats on the third size.

With Norwegian knitting, on the other hand, a pattern with an 18-stitch repeat may be repeated evenly across the round, but one size will use 13 repeats, the next size will contain 14 repeats, the third size will have 15 repeats, and so on. These basic patterns can be handled in three different ways:

* Begin each size at the same point in the chart and simply work the repeat to the end of the round.
* Using a particular stitch for the center front for all sizes, begin each size at a different spot in the repeat and then work the repeat to the end of the round, ending with a partial repeat.
* Begin the pattern at a different stitch for each size as the second version, then work the repeat to a stitch designated as the side stitch for the right-hand side of the body, and then work the back in the same way as the front.

Patterns worked in the first two methods are normally used only at the lower half of the body or, if used on the upper chest, are not placed directly at the shoulders.

In the first method, all sizes are begun at the same stitch in the repeat and will have a different part of the pattern at the center front and back. Only one or two sizes may have the same stitch at both the center of the front and back. However, the pattern for all sizes will end at the same point in the repeat (see Sample Norwegian Chart A).

In the second method, each size is started with a different stitch in the repeat. Reading the chart from right to left, the round is begun with the partial repeat, and then the 18-stitch repeat is worked to the end of the round, ending with a partial repeat that completes the repeat begun at the start of the round. As with the first example, only one or two sizes may have the same stitch at both the center of the front and back (see Sample Norwegian Chart B).

To avoid having a different stitch at the center of the front and back (especially at the shoulders where it will be obvious), as well as different center front/back stitches on each size, Norwegian patterns have solved this problem by dividing the body in half and placing markers for the left and right sides of the body. Using the same pattern stitch at the center of both the front and back for all sizes, a different starting point is indicated for each size (see Sample Norwegian Chart C).

In order to knit each round, begin at the left side of the body with the indicated stitch and work the partial repeat. Continue with the full repeat to the right side marker; you should end at the same point in the repeat as you had started to complete the front. Work the back in the same way as the front. The pattern on the front will mirror the pattern on the back, and the pattern on both the front and back will mirror on the left and right sides of the center and match at the shoulders.

Sample Norwegian Chart A

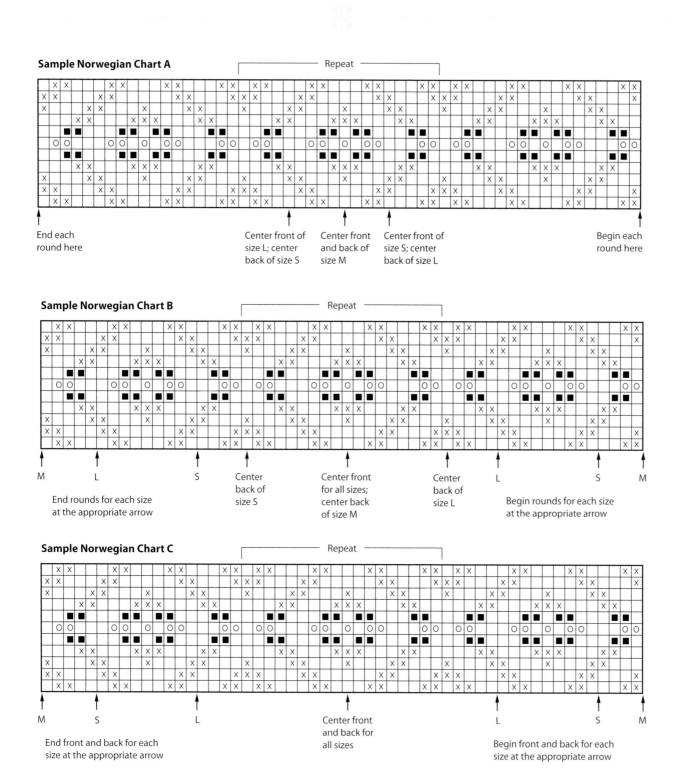

Repeat

End each round here

Center front of size L; center back of size S

Center front and back of size M

Center front of size S; center back of size L

Begin each round here

Sample Norwegian Chart B

Repeat

M L S

Center back of size S

Center front for all sizes; center back of size M

Center back of size L

L S M

End rounds for each size at the appropriate arrow

Begin rounds for each size at the appropriate arrow

Sample Norwegian Chart C

Repeat

M S L

Center front and back for all sizes

L S M

End front and back for each size at the appropriate arrow

Begin front and back for each size at the appropriate arrow

NONREPEATING PATTERNS

Similar to the basic pattern that is worked from side marker to side marker is the nonrepeating pattern. This type of pattern typically has a motif centered on both the front and back of the body, with elements that extend out toward the sides.

Charts for this type of design will show the entire front and back of the body. These sweaters are designed in one of two ways: with the same motifs placed on both the front and back of the body, with one chart to be used for both sides; or with different motifs for front and back, therefore needing a separate chart for each.

The illustration below shows how a chart would look for a design that is worked on both front and back. Begin by finding the starting point for the size you're making, and read the chart from right to left to the ending point for your size; you should have reached the halfway point of your round, and a side marker is typically placed here. In order to work the back of the body, begin again at the right side of the chart for your size and read to the left, ending again at the arrow for your size.

Half Body Chart

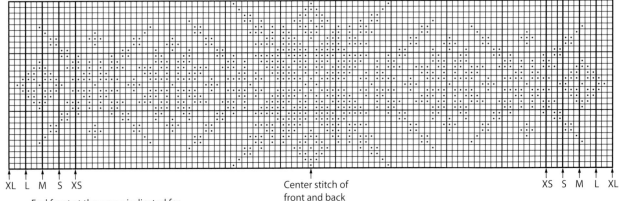

XL L M S XS   Center stitch of   XS S M L XL
                                                 front and back

End front at the arrow indicated for
chosen size, and then return to right side
of chart for the back. End back at the
arrow for chosen size.

Begin both front and back at the arrow
indicated for chosen size, and then
work from right to left to arrow at left
side of chart for chosen size.

This pattern will "break" at the sides of the body for most sizes. This is typical of many Norwegian designs, especially where the motifs are large and complex, or mirror from right to left on each side of a central motif. To avoid this break in the pattern at the sides of the body, some designs will insert a small, usually three- to five-stitch motif on each side of the body and underarm edge of the sleeves, or a purl stitch to act as a fake seam stitch. The Svale Pullover (on page 78) uses a fake seam stitch to divide the front and back patterns.

ALLOVER MIRRORED PATTERNS

Allover mirrored patterns are stunning designs and can be feats of pattern engineering. A large motif is often centered on the back (either at the neck and shoulders or at the bottom edge), with a ground pattern covering the majority of the body, and ending with another pattern at the center front. Since many of the sweaters featuring this type of design are cardigans, the pattern at the center front is frequently a small design that mirrors on each side of the opening, whether it has a crew-neck or V-neck.

Charts for these designs can be a bit tricky to read if you're not familiar with all the various styles of Norwegian designs (see the mirrored chart on the next page). However, don't let this deter you from attempting one of these beauties. As you'll discover, the main pattern on the body will most likely consist of a manageable repeat with special attention required when working the center of the front and back.

These charts are usually shown as the right half of the body, from the right front edge to the center back. To work from a chart like this, begin at the right-hand side of the chart and read from right to left to the center back stitch for the first half of the round. In order to complete the round, begin with the stitch on the chart *just to the right* of the center back stitch and read from left to right to the right-hand side of the chart.

SLEEVES

Patterns worked on the sleeves, especially large patterns or those placed at the top edges of a drop shoulder sleeve, are usually given in one of two versions. The first is the simple pattern repeat with the center stitch indicated. Because the number of stitches at the underarm edge is continually being increased as the sleeve grows longer, no starting point is indicated. In order to work this type of chart, determine the center of your round. Count back from the center stitch to the beginning of the round, and then count backward (from left to right) on the chart from the center stitch to find your starting point on that chart. It may be helpful to make several photocopies of the chart and piece them together so that you can mark the rounds where you need to increase and can see how to work the increases into the pattern.

The second version of the sleeve pattern is for a band worked at the top edge of the sleeve for a drop shoulder sweater. The chart will show a band the full width of the largest size, with the center indicated. As with the first sleeve version, determine the center of your round, and then count back from the center toward the right-hand side of the chart to find your starting point. It's an easy matter to mark your increases on the chart once you've determined the starting point.

NOTES ON COLOR STRANDING

There are many knitting traditions around the world that use color-stranded knitting, and a number of different ways of working with two or more colors. Some knitters work with the yarns held in their right hand, some in the left, and others favor a two-handed method. This last method is commonly referred to as the *Fair Isle method*, and is the one I prefer. Norwegian knitters hold both yarns in their left hand for Continental-style knitting. Use whichever method works best for you, or develop your own variation.

Mirrored Chart

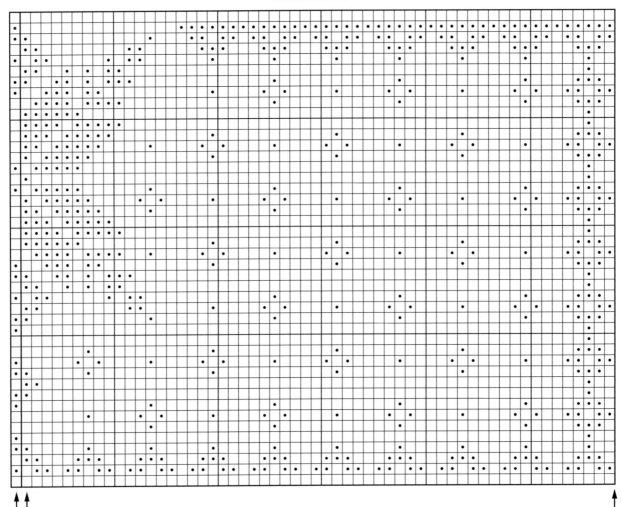

Begin here after working the
center stitch, and read chart
from left to right left side of body
and complete the round.

└─ Center stitch of Back

Begin right front here and read chart from right
to left, to center back. End left front here.

WHICH METHOD SHOULD I USE?

One reason why I like the two-handed method is that I can have a ball of yarn sitting on each side of me as I knit, so the yarn never tangles. I don't need to twist them every time I change colors or untwist tangled strands later. It also allows me to work more easily with three colors for a few rounds; I simply hold the third yarn in the hand with which I normally knit.

PUCKERING

Puckering is probably the most frustrating part of learning to strand colors; keeping the strands of yarn at a good tension when you first learn to knit with two colors can definitely be more art than science. Take a moment to look at how you hold the needles while you knit, and you'll see that stitches are bunched close to the ends of both needles. Whenever you need to change colors, spread the stitches apart slightly before knitting the next stitch with the new color.

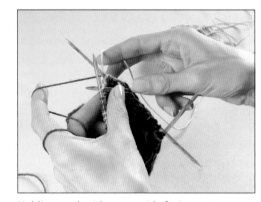

Holding work with wrong side facing out.

If you're still having a problem with puckering, try turning your work with the wrong side facing out—you'll still be knitting every round but the bulk of your work will be between you and the working ends of the needles. Working in this way, the yarn has just a little farther to travel along the outside of the piece than along the inside. Don't forget to spread your stitches apart each time you change colors. The stranded yarn should be straight but slightly relaxed across the wrong side, with the ends going up into the work and forming a slight *grin*.

When using double-pointed needles for sleeves and caps, if you have problems with puckering where the work changes from one needle to the next, add an additional needle into the work; the angle between needles will be wider with less chance of the stranded yarn pulling tight. I usually try to switch to a short, circular needle as soon as I can when knitting sleeves. You can use two short, circular needles if you don't like double-pointed needles, but be careful of the pattern puckering where you change from one needle to the next. There's only so much that blocking can do to fix puckering.

CHECKING YOUR TENSION AND GAUGE

As if stranding weren't enough to worry about, you also need to keep in mind that most knitters work their stranded color-work at a tighter tension than stockinette. It's always a good idea to work up both stockinette and colorwork swatches for any project that uses sizeable portions of both. Even if the pattern does not mention changing needle sizes as you change from stockinette to colorwork, and vice versa, you'll probably need to change at least one needle size to compensate for change in tension. If your colorwork is tighter than your stockinette, go up a size. The same advice applies if your colorwork should be looser—go down a needle size.

Knitting tension and gauge are such important aspects of knitting, and the finished piece so dependent on both, that they can't be emphasized enough. More ink and paper have probably been devoted to this issue than just about any other in knitting, yet some knitters continually refuse to knit gauge swatches. Some don't want to bother with swatches, some hate to knit them, and others don't see why they're needed. (I don't like to knit them but know how absolutely important they are!) If you don't knit gauge swatches, you shouldn't be surprised when things don't work out. Be sure to check your gauge often to avoid ugly surprises.

Another problem that can occur is the loose stitch at a change in colors. This tends to happen when, after changing colors, the unused strand carries over a fairly long distance before being used again. Two options for handling this are either tightening the strand slightly when you work the first stitch with that color, or weaving in the unused strand. I find the second method is helpful because it lets you tighten the stranded yarn just enough without getting it too tight.

CARRYING FLOATS

Just about everyone, whether or not they knit, is familiar with snagging a floated strand of yarn with jewelry, a finger, or a shirt button. Many Norwegian hand-knit sweaters have the same long floats across the wrong side. When worked in coarse wool, these strands will naturally felt together and you won't need to worry about snagging them. When worked in machine washable wools and smoother yarns, there won't be any felting, so you'll need to take that into consideration while knitting. As a general rule of thumb, make sure your floats are from $1/2$" (1.3cm) to $3/4$" (2cm) long, and certainly not more than 1" (2.5cm).

As far as the number of stitches that works out to, take your gauge into account; a finer yarn will have more stitches to the inch/centimeter than a heavier yarn, so you can float the yarn over more stitches before needing to twist or weave in the unused strand.

Two options for dealing with the stranded yarn are to twist the yarns every few stitches, or to weave them in. Twisting will cause the yarns to become tangled each round, and they will need to be untangled from time to time. This method is easiest to work when carrying both strands in the same hand.

The second method, weaving in the strands, is easiest to do when carrying one yarn in each hand. The quickest and simplest way of weaving in a strand (and the one most often shown in knitting books) is when the strand to be woven in is held in the left hand. Insert the right needle into the next stitch on the left needle as you would normally do to knit that stitch, making sure the yarn held in your left hand is held slightly above the right needle. Knit the stitch with the yarn in your right hand, and slip the stitch from the left needle. Bring the yarn in your left hand back to *normal* knitting position and work the next stitch (see photo A). When you take a look at the wrong side of your piece, the stranded yarn goes up slightly, then down, and is caught against the wrong side by the working strand.

Sometimes, when working with two or more colors in a round, it's necessary to weave in both strands on the same round. Weaving in the yarn carried in your right hand requires a little more finesse. There is a more *formal* way of working this move, but I've worked out my own variation that involves a bit less effort. In order to weave in the yarn stranded in your right hand, insert the right needle into the next stitch to work it as usual. Bring the yarn in your right hand around from the back of the work and lay it over the top of the left needle (see photos B and C); it may help if you hold it temporarily with your left thumb. Knit the stitch with the yarn in your left hand and, as you're bringing the right needle through to the right side with the new stitch, let the strand from your right hand slip to the back (see photo C). Make sure not to pull the right-hand strand through the loop as well, or you'll end up with two loops in the same stitch.

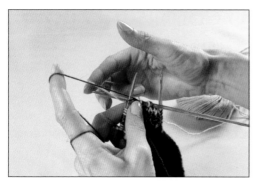

A. Weaving in the strand from the left hand.

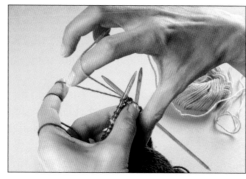

B. Bring yarn in your right hand over top left of the left needle.

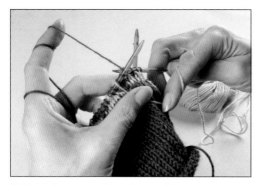

C. Hold the yarn to keep it out of the way.

D. When stitch has been knit, allow strand to return to the right.

When working stranded color knitting, and Norwegian knitting in particular, you'll encounter patterns with long stretches of one color that can span several rounds. You'll need to weave in the unused strand every round, but you don't want to use the same spot each time as this will result in the color showing through on the right side with a *ladder* effect. Instead, stagger the point where you weave in the stranded yarn each round.

Some knitters don't like their floats to be longer than one or two stitches. Weaving in strands every other stitch, or every third stitch, will produce a very heavy and stiff fabric with a lot of the color showing through on the right side. This method also uses more yarn; it may not seem like it while knitting, but the yarn being woven in will need to travel up and down quite a bit. This can mean running out of a color. If you're knitting from a pattern that requires that technique, the extra amount of yarn is already calculated into the amounts stated at the beginning of the pattern. However, if the pattern does not specifically tell you to weave in that frequently, keep in mind that you're more than likely going to need additional yarn.

Working with More than Two Colors in a Round

Most stranded patterns are worked with two colors. That being said, with Norwegian knitting patterns it quickly becomes obvious that there are patterns using three or four colors in a round. You have several options for handling all those strands of yarn.

If you strand yarn by holding one yarn in each hand for two-color patterns, carry the third color in the hand with which you're most comfortable working. If you carry two yarns in the same hand, you can carry more than two strands in that same hand. Another option is to simply let the extra color hang off the wrong side of your work, then bring it up each time you need to use that color.

Devices called *knitting thimbles* (or yarn guides) are available to help control multiple strands of yarn; tension can become particularly tricky to control when working with three or more strands of yarn, so investing in one of these relatively inexpensive tools makes sense for a beginning stranding knitter. It holds from two to four strands of yarn and can help with controlling tension, even if you're just using it for a single strand in two-handed stranding. Two basic styles of knitting thimbles can be found in yarn shops and by mail order.

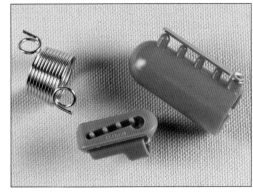

Knitting thimbles.

One version of the thimble has a plastic ring fitting over the index finger, or a tip that fits over the tip of the finger, and small posts hold the yarns in place between each post. This style is worn so that the yarns are held running over the top of the finger.

The second thimble style is a metal coil with a ring at each end; this style is commonly called a *Norwegian knitting thimble* (or strickfingerhut). The coil is slid onto the index finger with the rings in the front of the index finger so that one yarn is fed over the top of the finger and the one near the tip feeds under the finger.

If you do not want to strand more than two colors at a time, try working with just the background color and main pattern color. Extra colors can be added in later using duplicate stitch, also known as *Swiss darning*. This technique is very handy for filling in a third color used for only a few stitches. When used over a large area, however, that section of the knitted fabric becomes very stiff and won't lie flat, especially around the edges of the duplicate stitched area.

Plastic thimble in use.

Metal coil thimble in use.

CHAPTER 8

Creating a Hem

The hem of a knit garment can be simple or elaborate, knitted with the main part of the garment or added later, ribbed, textured, or worked in stockinette or a color pattern. It can be a single layer or with a facing turned to the wrong side. Regardless of how a hem is made, it should always complement the body of the garment.

The patterns in this book feature a range of hem treatments. Several designs feature either a knit 1, purl 1 or a knit 2, purl 2 rib for a more traditional, fitted bottom edge. Garter stitch is used for an uncomplicated treatment for a casual look but can also be used effectively for the lower edge of a more sophisticated piece such as the Bouclé Mohair Cardigan (see page 100). Just three rows of garter at the lower edge of the Sonora Tunic (see page 89) echo the pattern in the body and allow the lower edge to scallop with the pattern. Garter rib will give you the look of a wider rib if you don't want it to pull in along the lower edge.

HEM EDGING

A hem edge that starts right into the pattern is often effective for cabled or lace patterns, especially when the pattern naturally creates a shaped edge. A sweater that starts out right away with stockinette will have a rolled edge and casual appearance.

Another way to use stockinette at the lower edge of a garment is in a faced hem. A wider hem will have more weight and tend to hang straighter than a very narrow-faced hem, which may have a tendency to curl above the sewn edge. The look can be casual and sporty, crisp and polished, feminine, or childlike and sweet, depending on the yarn. You can add a narrow band of stranded color pattern to the outside of a faced hem, and the facing will cover the back of the stranded area (and no floated strands of yarn to snag).

If you're adding a faced hem, one drawback is a tendency for the lower edge to flare out; this usually happens if the same-size needle is used to knit the facing as the edge above where the hem is turned, or the same number of stitches is used for both parts of the hem. You can keep that from happening by doing one of the following.

❋ **First option:** Cast on the facing stitches using smaller needles. Knit the facing, and then work the desired turning row. Change to the larger needles for the body of the sweater, and begin the main part of the knitting. A drawstring or elastic cord can be threaded through the hem to adjust the lower edge and add a contemporary touch.

❋ **Second option:** Cast facing stitches onto smaller needles. Instead of working stockinette, work a knit 1, purl 1 rib for just about the entire length of the facing. Work one or two rows of stockinette, and then work a turning row. Then you're set to change needle sizes and begin working on the right side.

❋ **Third option:** Cast on about 5 percent fewer stitches than will be needed for the body. Knit the facing, and then work a turning row. Work one more row of stockinette and increase to the appropriate number of stitches for the main part of the body. Change to the larger-size needles.

❋ **Fourth option:** This method was used for the Zara Cardigan (see page 95). Begin working on the main part of the body after casting stitches onto the larger needle size. Once the body is finished, you'll need to pick up stitches along the lower edge with a smaller needle and finer yarn to make the edging and facing along the lower edge of the body. You'll be picking up more stitches with the finer yarn than were originally cast on to compensate for the difference in gauges between the two yarns. A variation on this would be to use the finer yarn and smaller needles to cast on more stitches than needed for the body. Work the facing, and then turn the row and bottom edge of the piece. Change to heavier yarn and larger needles, and when working the first row, decrease to the required number of stitches. Now you're set to work the main part of the piece.

TURNING ROWS

An important part of the look of the faced edge, whether it's a hem or an edging along a front opening or armhole, is the *turn row* or *fold line*. This row, as the name implies, is where the edge will be folded so that the facing can be sewn down. The facing will be worked as part of the main piece. In the case of button bands and trims where stitches are picked up along a vertical or horizontal edge, the turn row is usually worked when the band has reached the required length.

My favorite turning row is a simple row of reverse stockinette (purled on the right side, or knit on the wrong side). The edge is simple and clean, and it can be worked over any number of stitches.

A second common turn row is the picot edge. This row is most often worked on the right side but can also be done on the wrong side. When working in the round, make sure to have an even number of stitches, and work it in this fashion:

*yo, k2tog; repeat from * to the end of the round.

In order to work this row flat, you'll need to have an odd number of stitches so that the ends of the piece are identical. When worked flat, work the row in this manner:

k1, *yo, k2tog; repeat from * to the end. It may also be worked *k2tog, yo; repeat from * to the last stitch and end k1. And to work either version on the wrong side, change the k2tog to p2tog and purl the extra stitches at the beginning or end of the row.

Falk Cardigan hem.

Picot hem on the Svale Pullover.

Another way to work an edge with a facing is to simply knit until the piece measures the depth of both the hem and the facing, and place a removable stitch marker or safety pin in the edge where the facing is to be turned to the wrong side. When finishing the piece, turn the edge to the inside where the marker or safety pin had been placed. A variation on this method is to work the row where the facing will be turned with a needle two sizes larger than the needles used for the hem. After that row, immediately go back to the correct needle size for the next row. The wider row will form a natural turning edge.

A row of reverse stockinette used as the turn row on the Heilo Pullover's zipper placket.

CHAPTER **9**

Armhole Options

Sweaters made using the *drop shoulder armhole* are probably the easiest to work; there's no shaping done while knitting, and work progresses directly to the neckline or shoulders. The armholes for a drop shoulder sweater need extra depth to accommodate the additional bulk of the seam and facing at the bottom of the armhole. A *square armhole* involves either binding off all of the stitches for the armhole at each side of the body on one round, or slipping them to a stitch holder, although this is more commonly used with Fair Isle than Norwegian sweaters. A square armhole can be shallower than one needed for the drop shoulder armhole. Requiring further shaping, and therefore being more involved to work, is the *shaped armhole*. A shaped armhole can be more fitted to provide a more flattering look.

All three styles can be worked in the round, with cutting stitches added to the square and shaped versions after removing stitches at the bottom of the armhole. This makes colorwork patterns easier to knit, as you're always working from the right side. How each armhole style is worked does vary.

DROP SHOULDER ARMHOLES

Armholes for drop shoulder pullovers and cardigans are not formed while knitting. These armholes are typically deep and used for sweaters that can be worn with other garments layered under them, making them ideal for outdoor wear. The extra bulk created by the facings and seams in deep armholes won't bind under the arm. The additional room in the sleeves also allows for ease of movement. Overall, the look of these garments is casual or sporty, and the armhole for a classic ski sweater falls into this category.

Heilo Pullover armhole.

The finished depth of the drop shoulder armhole is very easy to adjust since it's determined by the width of the sleeve below the facing. It will be very important to make sure both sleeves are the same width before you mark the depth for the armhole on the body.

When making a sweater with drop shoulders, you'll need to use stitch markers at the sides of the body, as already mentioned in chapter 7. This is especially important when patterns repeat across each round without breaking at the side markers. These markers also serve as handy reference points for placement of patterns and neck shaping. When binding off the shoulder stitches, replace the stitch markers with removable markers or safety pins in the bound-off edge.

With sweaters using patterns that break at the side markers, it can be easier to see where the stitch markers had been placed by where the pattern breaks. But, it's still a good idea to place removable markers at the shoulder edges for the quick visual reference they create around the armhole.

Machine stitching to secure the yarns before cutting is usually done two stitches away from the line running down from the shoulder where the marker was placed. The sleeve is sewn into the armhole one stitch away from the machine stitching, leaving a three-stitch seam allowance. Each completed armhole opening will be a total of six stitches wide.

The top of the sleeve for the drop shoulder sweater is straight across, with no shaping after the required length is reached. Several rounds of reverse stockinette are added to the top of this sleeve for a facing.

SHAPED ARMHOLES

On the other end of the spectrum is the shaped armhole. Shaping is done along the lower edges of this armhole and eliminates some of the bulk at the underarm edge of the sleeve and bottom of the armhole found on drop shoulder styles.

The shaping can be worked as simply as binding off most of the stitches at the bottom of the opening and then decreasing one stitch every other row until the required number of shoulder stitches is reached. Cutting stitches are added on the round following the bind-off to begin the armhole. This type of shaped armhole results in an angled shape and is often used on Fair Isle and other colorwork sweaters that require some armhole shaping.

Ambrosia Vest armhole.

For a more contoured fit and an armhole that often comes much closer to the armpit without binding, the initial bind-off removes fewer stitches, and multiple stitches are bound off every other row, in decreasing quantities. The curve at the bottom of the armhole resembles the armhole of a blouse or jacket.

Because the bottom of the armhole has a curved edge, several rows will need to be worked back and forth before adding cutting stitches and resuming work in the round. The reason? Binding off multiple stitches leaves a hole in the knitting, and machine stitching to secure the yarn will be awkward at best. In addition, you'll have an uneven seam allowance to deal with later. You'll need to work about 4 to 10 rows back and forth, and bind off the required multiple stitches at the beginning of each row to shape each armhole. Once you can start decreasing one stitch each time, add the cutting stitches and resume working in the round.

One advantage to this method is that when picking up stitches for the facing later, you'll only be working along straight and angled edges and won't need to deal with the curved edge or increase stitches to fit the facing around the bottom of the armhole. Any bulk that might result from adding a facing at the bottom of an armhole that sits directly under the arm is eliminated.

The sleeve fitting into this armhole doesn't need to be as wide as that of a drop shoulder sweater; a shaped sleeve cap can be added so that the total length along the shaped edge equals the shaped edge of the armhole. After the sleeve has been sewn into the armhole, the facing stitches are picked up only along the cut edge of the armhole to work the facing.

SQUARE ARMHOLES

Somewhere between the drop shoulder and the shaped armhole is the square armhole. There's a slight reduction in the bulk at the bottom of the armhole of a drop shoulder sweater, and it is simpler to work than the shaped armhole. Like the first version of the shaped armhole described earlier, the cutting stitches are added on the round after the initial bind-off. After adding the cutting stitches, however, no further shaping is done because all the stitches for the armhole are removed at one time.

Sleeve caps for this armhole style are worked back and forth for a distance equal to half the width of the number of stitches bound off. A facing is then added after the sleeve reaches its finished length and will cover only the cut edges along the sides of the armhole.

Daylily Cardigan armhole.

AN ARMHOLE VARIATION

What if your sweater calls for a drop shoulder and you decide, when you're ready to begin shaping the neckline, that you want a shaped armhole instead? The most obvious answer would be to rip back to the desired armhole depth and reknit. If you're not inclined to do that, why not continue working as you would for the drop shoulder style, and then when you're ready to do the finishing, sew in the shape of your shaped armhole and cut it open?

The technique would be similar to that used for a sewn-and-cut neckline. Unlike the shaped armhole that has been worked in the knitting, when using this version you would need to include a facing around the entire armhole. This armhole would need to be slightly deeper than you might use for a shaped armhole without a facing.

Who was it who said every mistake is a design opportunity? Well, it's not exactly a mistake, but every knitter has the right to change her or his mind. By learning the techniques in this book, you can do just that!

CHAPTER 10

Shaping the Neckline

Whether you choose to work in the round to the shoulder, or bind off at the bottom of the front neck edge, there are numerous options on how you can shape the neck of a sweater. When you knit straight to the shoulder, mark your neck opening, and then sew and cut it open, you've multiplied your options—choose a crewneck or V-neck, or anything in between, or leave the edge uncut for a boatneck. For sweaters with bound-off neck edges, you can work back and forth or add cutting stitches so that you can continue working in the round.

The boatneck pullover is about as basic as you can get when it comes to necklines. No shaping is involved and elaborate color patterns can continue directly to the shoulder without interruption. The neck width and shoulder width on each side of the body are specified in the pattern, so all you need to do is make sure colorwork patterns match at the shoulders when you sew it all together.

Crew, square, and V-necks can all be worked in three different ways:

* Shaped by binding off the center front stitches, and then working the rest of the body back and forth.

* Shaped by binding off the center front stitches, casting on cutting stitches, and continuing in the round.

* Knitting all the way to the shoulder, without shaping.

In the last variation, the front and back necklines are marked after binding off all stitches. Machine stitching secures the yarns so that the neck can be cut after adding the neckband. The discussion that follows covers how to work the first two neck options, and the actual sewing and cutting of the third option will be covered more extensively in chapter 16.

NECKLINES SHAPED BY WORKING BACK AND FORTH

PULLOVERS

Let's begin with the most obvious fact about pullovers that are knit in the round: All rounds are begun and ended at the left side of the body, with the front stitches being worked before the back. Now with that out of the way, when it comes time to begin shaping the front neck edge, the initial set of stitches bound off will be one-quarter of the way across the round.

To begin the neck, work the stitches for the left side of the front, bind off the given number of stitches for the front neck, and then work to the end of the round (across the stitches for the right front and all the stitches of the back), and end there.

On the majority of Norwegian pullovers, there's a colorwork pattern at the shoulders. You'll need to keep that in mind as you approach the neckline. When there's color patterning at the shoulders, you can't simply knit to the front neck edge to continue the shaping. If you just work the pattern from the left side to the front neck, there will be two rows of the same pattern on the left shoulder. The simplest solutions are to add cutting stitches, or to shift stitches so that rows begin and end at the front neck.

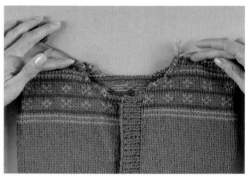

Cardigan neckline that was shaped working back and forth.

If you're concerned about working color charts from the wrong side or your tension as you purl with two or more colors, the distance from the beginning of the neckline to the shoulder is relatively short. You can always add cutting stitches to continue working in the round. Intricate patterns and differences between knit row and purl row tension would be good reasons for adding cutting stitches. Typically, though, patterns at the shoulders tend to be simpler and the distance from the beginning of the neck to shoulders is short, so it's easy to work many of those sweaters back and forth from this point.

Once you've reached the end of the round after working the initial bind-off of stitches for the front neck, cut the yarns and leave tails long enough to weave in. Slip the left-front shoulder stitches (from the beginning of the round to the left edge of the front neck) from your left needle to the right needle. Both ends of your circular needle will now be at the front neck opening. Reattach the yarns, and then begin working back and forth. Whether you begin with a right side row or wrong side row usually doesn't matter, and would be stated in the pattern instructions if important to the design.

Now that you're working back and forth, work continues across one front shoulder, across the back, and then across the remaining front shoulder. Multiple stitches are bound off at the beginning of each row for further neck shaping (at the beginning of right side rows for the right edge, and at the beginning of wrong side rows for the left edge). Once you've reached a point where only one stitch at a time is decreased on each side, those stitches can be decreased at the beginning and end of every other (usually right side) row, by simply knitting them together at the edges. The beauty of working shoulders in this way is that you're still working over the entire body and won't need to work the front and back separately.

When you've reached the beginning of the back neck, the row will be divided in this way: Work the front and back shoulder stitches on one half of the body, bind off the center back stitches to begin shaping the back neck edge, and then work the stitches for the front and back shoulders on the other half of the body. If you'd like, you can attach another ball of yarn before shaping the back neck, and work on both shoulders at the same time.

From this point, work over both the front and back of each shoulder until the finished length is reached. Back neck shaping is done on right side rows for the left neck edge, and on wrong side rows for the right neck edge. Occasionally, however, there is no back neck shaping. In that case, simply continue over all the stitches until the finished length is reached, and then bind off all stitches.

CARDIGANS

Cardigan crew necklines that are shaped by knitting back and forth are worked a bit differently; the rounds already begin and end at the center front instead of the left side. The easiest method to use when beginning a cardigan neckline is to end the last round the stated number of stitches before the end of that round and the cutting stitches. Bind off the cutting stitches and the given number of stitches on each side of the cutting stitches to begin the neck. For example, a pattern may say to end the last round 10 stitches before the cutting stitches. As cutting stitches are typically 4 stitches wide and rounds begin and end at the center of the cutting stitches, you'll actually be ending the round 12 stitches before the end of the round (2 cutting stitches + the last 10 stitches of the round).

Bind off 24 stitches (10 stitches before the cutting stitches + the 4 cutting stitches + 10 stitches after the cutting stitches), and then work in the pattern until you get back to the left edge of the front neck. You're then ready to begin working back and forth in the same way as for pullovers (described earlier). No need, though, to cut yarns and shift stitches as you would for pullovers. The back neck opening, though, is shaped in the same way as for pullovers.

NECKLINES SHAPED IN THE ROUND

PULLOVERS

If you don't want to work the pullover neck back and forth, you can add cutting stitches and avoid cutting the yarn and shifting stitches because the rounds will still begin and end at the left side of the body. However, you will be limited to single-stitch decreases after the initial set of stitches are bound off for the same reasons as shaped armholes, resulting in a neckline that's angled rather than curved. These necklines are often shallower and the initial bind-off is worked over more stitches.

To begin a neckline that will be shaped in the round, work the left side stitches, bind off the stitches to begin the neck opening, work the right side of the body and then the back, and end at the left side of the body. The next round is worked by continuing the pattern across the left shoulder, adding cutting stitches in the space above the bound-off stitches and then working to the end of the round. Decrease one stitch on each side of the cutting stitches every other round (or sometimes every round); because the decreases would be hidden by the neckband, the decreases can be done however you like.

The back neck opening can also be shaped using cutting stitches so that you can continue working in the round, and would be worked in the same way as the front neck opening. Since the back neck opening is often less than 1" (2.5cm) deep, and sometimes as shallow as $1/2$" (1.5cm), it would be easier to work the back neck opening back and forth for such a short length.

To work back and forth after binding off the center back stitches and adding cutting stitches at the front neck opening, slip the left back shoulder stitches (from the end of the round to the left edge of the back neck) from your right needle to the left needle. Both ends of your circular needle will be at the back neck opening. Reattach the yarns, and then begin working back and forth.

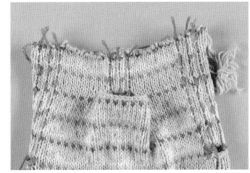

Square neckline that was shaped by working in the round after the initial bind off.

CARDIGANS

Necklines shaped in the round for cardigans begin in the same way as necklines worked back and forth: by ending the last round the stated number of stitches before the end of that round. Bind off the number of stitches stated in the pattern, and then knit all the way across the round to the left-neck edge. Cast on the cutting stitches, and then join to the other side of the neck. Further shaping of the neck is worked in the same way as for pullover necklines shaped in the round. The options for shaping the back neckline are the same as for pullovers.

SQUARE AND V-NECK LINES

Both square and V-neck lines can be worked either back and forth or in the round, as described for both pullovers and cardigans.

Square necklines typically bind off all stitches for the full width of the neck opening at one time. The bind-off round for a square neckline is worked the same as for crewneck pullovers and cardigans. If worked back and forth, the left shoulder stitches are shifted over to the right needle, and work continues without further shaping. If work is to progress in the round, add the cutting stitches, and continue up to the shoulder.

V-neck pullovers that are worked back and forth to shape the front neck are similar to crewnecks. After binding off one or two stitches for the bottom of the neck opening (the actual number depends on whether there are an odd or even number of stitches for the front), shift the stitches for the left front as you would for a crewneck pullover. Work then progresses the same as for a crewneck pullover.

For V-neck pullovers with neck shaping worked in the round, the center stitch(es) are bound off, and then cutting stitches are added so that work can continue in the round. Because only one or two stitches are bound off and four cutting stitches are added, the lower end of the cutting stitches will bunch at the opening while working, but will flatten once cut.

Front neck shaping for both square and V-neck cardigans is worked the same as crewneck cardigans. The only variations are the number of stitches initially bound off and how the remaining shaping is done.

Square neck that has been worked back and forth.

V-neck that has been worked back and forth.

V-neck that has been worked in the round.

SEWN AND CUT NECKLINES

All the necklines that have already been discussed can also be sewn and cut without any shaping while doing the actual knitting, except boatneck edges which, of course, don't get any shaping at all.

A nice thing about this neckline is that you can customize the depth and width of the neck if desired. Remember, though, to take into account any pattern across the upper body or around the neck opening that may need to be altered. When deciding how wide and deep to make the neck, always make sure that the size is sufficient to fit over the wearer's head. This may sound a bit too obvious to state, but it's better to measure twice and cut once; after it's been cut, there's no going back unless you want to make it wider.

CHAPTER 11

What to Do with the Shoulders

E ven if you have a favorite way to join the shoulders of your sweaters, there are some intriguing ways that Norwegian shoulder joining can be worked that are well worth learning. You can choose either one of the three methods that utilize live stitches or a fourth method using whipstitch after the shoulder stitches are bound off. All these methods produce practical and decorative seams that are also very stable.

THREE-NEEDLE BIND-OFF

This technique, which is commonly used in Norwegian knitting, is also frequently used in many book and magazine patterns and is discussed in this book because it is so useful. The seams are placed on either the right or wrong side; the right side produces a decorative ridge.

For this method, you'll need to slip the front shoulder stitches to one needle and the back shoulder stitches to a second needle (double-pointed needles work well for this). Hold both needles with the right sides together (you'll be looking at the wrong sides of both). If you have a particularly deep armhole, a deep-neck opening, or are making a cardigan that has the front edge already cut open, then it's a good idea at this time to make sure that the front is not twisted and that both neck edges are at the same end.

Holding the third needle in your right hand, insert it into the first stitch on both needles, wrap the yarn around the needle to knit the stitches, and draw the loop through both stitches and slide them off the left needles—you'll have one stitch on your right needle. *Knit two more stitches together in the same manner. Lift the first stitch you made over the top of the second stitch and off the tip of the right needle—one stitch remains. Repeat from * until all the stitches from both left needles have been knitted together, and then fasten off the remaining stitch.

Three-needle bind-off shown in both photos.

If you want the bound-off ridge to show on the right side, hold the needles with the wrong sides together before beginning to bind off. You can work from armhole to neck, or the other way around on both shoulders. But if you want the stitches to face the same direction on both shoulders, one shoulder will need to be worked from armhole to neck and the other from neck to armhole, with the same side of the body facing you while working both seams.

SHOULDER JOIN WORKED FROM LIVE STITCHES SLIPPED TO THE SAME NEEDLE

Here's another shoulder join that can be worked on either the right or wrong side. It's great to know this technique if both sets of stitches are on holders and you don't have a third needle handy, or are simply looking for another way to bind off the shoulders. The appearance is much the same as the three-needle bind-off.

Hold both front and back shoulder stitches of the same side of the body in your left hand, with the right (or wrong) sides together, making sure nothing is twisted and neck edges are on the same end. Hold another needle in your right hand. Slip a stitch from the front set of stitches to the right needle purlwise, then one stitch from the back set of stitches to the right needle purlwise, and then repeat, alternating front and back each time until all stitches are on the same needle.

Hold the needle with the stitches in your left hand and a second needle in your right hand. *Lift the second stitch on the left needle up and over the first stitch, and off the needle. Knit the first stitch and leave that stitch on the right needle. Repeat from * again—you have two stitches on the right needle. Lift the first stitch on the right needle up and over the second stitch to bind off one—one stitch remains on the right needle. Continue working across all the remaining stitches on the left needle until they have all been bound off, and then fasten off the remaining stitch (see the photos on the next page).

Slipping stitches to the same needle.

Lifting second stitch over the first on the left needle.

Knitting the stitch on the left needle.

Lifting the first stitch on the right needle over second.

TWO-NEEDLE BIND-OFF WITH LIVE STITCHES ON BOTH NEEDLES

This technique can be worked in three variations. The first version of this bind-off is the original Norwegian way. The second version resulted when I misread a literal translation of the method. Both of these variations are interesting and really quite easy to do once you get the hang of working with live stitches on both needles. The third version came about when I was trying to be too clever in figuring out what the translation was saying.

VERSION 1

Version 1 has the look of a grafted seam but has the stability needed for a shoulder, or any other seam supporting weight. The bound-off stitches form two parallel chains running perpendicular to the stitches along either side of the seam on the wrong side.

To work Version 1 (see the photos below), hold a needle with live stitches in each hand and with the working yarn at the tip of the right needle. Insert the right needle into the first two stitches on the left needle purlwise, and purl these two stitches together. Slip the resulting stitch back to the left needle so the right leg of the stitch faces the front. Insert the left needle into the front loops of the first two stitches on the right needle. Wrap the yarn around the left needle, from the front up over the top and between both needles, and purl the two stitches together. Slip the resulting loop back to the right needle, making sure the left leg of the stitch faces the front. Continue to purl two stitches together across both edges, alternating left needle, then right needle until the last two stitches on the right needle have been worked—you'll have two stitches remaining on the left needle. Lift the back stitch up and over the last stitch worked and off the needle. Fasten off the remaining stitch.

This method tends to twist the stitches from the right needle when worked with the stitches on the right needle "as is" after completing the shoulder. If you want the stitches for both sides of the seam to be untwisted, before beginning to bind off make sure all stitches on the right needle are situated with the left leg of each stitch in the front.

Purling two stitches together on the left needle.

Purling two stitches together on the right needle.

The finished seam.

The finished seam from the wrong side.

VERSION 2

To work Version 2, hold a needle with live stitches in each hand as directed for Version 1, and make sure the working yarn is at the tip of the right needle and held to the back. Insert the right needle through the backs of the loops of the first two stitches on the left needle knitwise, and knit these two stitches together. Slip the resulting stitch back to the left needle so the right leg of the stitches faces the front. Insert the left needle into the back of the loops for the first two stitches on the right needle. Wrap the yarn around the left needle, over the top and between both needles, and knit the two stitches together. Slip the resulting loop back to the right needle, making sure the right leg of the stitch faces the front. Continue to knit two stitches together across both edges, alternating left needle, then right needle until the last two stitches on the right needle have been worked—you'll have two stitches remaining on the left needle. Lift the back stitch up and over the stitch at the tip of the needle. Fasten off the remaining stitch.

　　This method tends to twist the stitches from the left needle with the stitches on the left needle when worked with the stitches "as is" after completing the shoulder but is barely visible under the line of chain stitches when using this method. However, if you still want the stitches for both sides of the seam to be untwisted, before beginning to bind off make sure all stitches on the left needle are situated with the left leg of each stitch in the front.

Knitting two stitches together on the left needle.

Knitting two stitches together on the right needle.

The finished seam on the right side.

VERSION 3

This variation creates an interesting ridge along the seam and can be a bit tricky to work. For Version 3, it's not important which direction each leg of each stitch faces, as each of the stitches will *lay on their sides*.

So to work Version 3, hold a needle with live stitches in each hand as directed for Version 1, and make sure the working yarn is at the tip of the right needle. Insert the right needle into the first two stitches on the left needle *from left to right through the backs of both loops (purlwise)*, and purl these two stitches together. Slip the resulting stitch back to the left needle. Insert the left needle into the first two stitches on the right needle *from right to left through the backs of both loops (purlwise)*. Wrap the yarn around the left needle, and purl the two stitches together. Slip the resulting loop back to the right needle. Continue to purl two stitches together across both edges, alternating left needle, then right needle until the last two stitches on the right needle have been worked—you'll have two stitches remaining on the left needle. Lift the back stitch up and over the other stitch and off the needle. Fasten off the remaining stitch.

Purling two stitches together through the back of the loops on the left needle.

Purling two stitches together through the back of the loops on the right needle.

The finished seam.

WHIPSTITCHED SEAM

This seam is another commonly used method of joining shoulders of Norwegian sweaters. The resulting edge is simple, decorative, and quite stable. It lies flat and the edges are neat on the wrong side. Unlike grafting the shoulder stitches together or using backstitches to sew a shoulder seam, there's no need to keep your stitches even. The yarn used to sew the seam is pulled tight to draw the edges together securely, thus preventing the seam from stretching.

After reaching the finished body length, the last row of each shoulder is purled from the right side (or knit from the wrong side if the next row happens to be a wrong side row). Bind off in stockinette on the next row; when cutting the yarn after binding off, you may wish to leave an end long enough to sew the shoulder seam (about twice the length of the seam). The shoulders are sewn together once the machine stitching for the armholes has been done and the armholes have been cut open.

Holding the shoulders together before beginning seam.

Stitching the seam.

The finished seam on the right side.

The finished seam on the wrong side.

At this point, take a look at the bound-off edges you'll be working with. The purl row left a set of bumps on the right side of your work. You'll be sewing the seam through the set of bumps pointing toward the bound-off edge, leaving the other set of bumps (pointing toward the body) visible on the right side. Students in the classes I've taught have referred to these as *smiles* and *frowns,* or *innies* and *outies,* and both descriptions are accurate. Keep in mind that you're going to completely ignore the bound-off edge, which rolls to the inside as you sew the seam.

Hold the front and back of the same shoulder edge to edge, with the right side facing and the ends facing each other. Thread a yarn needle with the strand of yarn. Insert the needle through the first bumps at the edge, and pull the yarn through. Taking a second stitch through the same two bumps will secure the end. Bring the needle back to the same side of the shoulder where the first stitch was started so the yarn will go over the top of the seam. *Insert the needle through the next bumps, making sure to go through in the same direction as you had for the first stitch. Draw the yarn through and tighten it a bit as you go. Repeat from * until you reach the end of the shoulder.

Once you've reached the machine stitching at the armhole, the last stitch can be in the last bumps before the machine stitching. If there's a little space between the rows of machine stitching, you can work the last stitch here as well. Take a second stitch through the last stitch to secure the end of the seam, and then knot the yarn—this end can be woven in when you complete the sleeve seams.

Two important points to bear in mind when sewing this shoulder seam are to always insert the needle into the seam in the same direction for each stitch, and to sew only the purl bumps that face each other, leaving the lower purl bumps to show on the right side.

CHAPTER 12

Sleeves and Sleeve Facings

In this chapter, I'll be going over a number of options on how sleeve facings and their joined armholes are treated in a variety of applications. Knitted facings can be added to the tops of the drop shoulder and square armholes while making the sleeves. The shaped armhole can also have a knitted facing, although it's added after the sleeve has been sewn into the armhole. Braid or ribbon can be sewn on as an alternative to the knitted facing, especially if the sweater is knit in a heavy yarn.

FOR DROP SHOULDER SWEATERS

The drop shoulder sweater is probably the first thing that comes to mind when anyone mentions Norwegian sweaters. It's a common sweater silhouette and is uncomplicated to knit. Since the armhole needs to be cut open, a facing on the sleeve is an extremely important component of the sleeve and is normally added at the top after the required sleeve length has been reached. This facing is usually worked in the last color or last background color that was used for the main part of the sleeve. One round of stockinette is worked, and then the facing is worked in reverse stockinette. It's usually four to six rounds high but can be more if needed. You can knit the rounds instead of purling them, by turning the sleeve with the wrong side facing out in order to knit each round.

There are a couple of important points to keep in mind with this style of armhole. First, the facing will need to cover the entire cut edge around the armhole, including the bottom of the opening. To do this, you'll need to increase stitches at the beginning and end of every other round to add the extra width needed to go around the bottom of the armhole. If those extra stitches are not added, the seam would bunch up at the underarm and not fit properly. Second, there is usually a pattern centered on the sleeve and will need to be centered at the shoulder seam when attaching the sleeve to the body of the sweater. The armhole seam will be started at the shoulder to ensure the pattern on the sleeve is centered.

RATIO OF ROWS TO STITCHES

Another consideration when sewing in the sleeves is the ratio of rows (in the depth of the armhole) to the number of stitches (at the top of the sleeve). The gauge being rectangular rather than square, every stitch along the top of the sleeve will be sewn through, although not every row on the body will be stitched into. For example, a cardigan may have 111 stitches across the top of the sleeve (below the facing), and an armhole of 9" (23cm).

If the pattern has a stitch gauge of 24 stitches per 4" (10cm), the actual circumference of the top of the sleeve will be 18½" (47cm). Because the underarm edge of the sleeve also needs to go around the bottom of the armhole, you will need to cover the bottom of the armhole about 1" (2.5cm).

When calculating the ratio, I subtract 5 stitches from the sleeve total so that I won't need to stretch the sleeve to fit around the bottom of the armhole and keep a 9" (23cm) deep armhole: 111 – 5 = 106 stitches to go around the sides of the armhole; half of those stitches will be on the front and the remaining half on the back, so 106 ÷ 2 = 53 stitches will lie to both the front and back.

If my row gauge was 28 rows per 4" (10cm), for a 9" (23cm) deep armhole, my armhole would be 63 rows deep. Add 1 row to account for the extra row needed for a seam allowance at the bottom of the armhole (63 + 1 = 64 rows).

Next, to find the number of rows I need to sew into before skipping a row, I find the difference between both numbers (64 – 53 = 11), which means I need to skip a total of 11 rows over the 64 rows in the armhole, 1 at a time at specific intervals along the length of the armhole.

Because 11 doesn't go evenly into 64, I'll need to vary the number of rows between each row skipped. In this case, it works out that if I sew into 4 rows, skip the next row, sew into 5 rows, skip the next row, and repeat this sequence 5 times ([4 + 1 + 5 + 1] × 5 = 55), I end up sewing into 4 rows, skipping 1, and then sewing into 4 rows at the bottom of the armhole (the extra 9 rows I need to cover: 55 + 9 = 64). As you sew the seam, the numbers can be *fudged* a bit as you work, though do make sure the pattern is centered at the shoulder, and the sleeve is evenly sewn into the armhole.

METHODS FOR SEWING SLEEVES INTO DROP ARMHOLES

The sleeves are normally sewn into the armholes using mattress stitch, or a variation of it, depending on where you sew into the sleeve and the desired appearance of the resulting seam. The hand sewing on the body of the sweater will be done through the first stitch/row in from the machine stitching, so that the machine stitching is between the seam you're sewing and the cut edge. On the sleeves, it can be worked below the facing, or into the very bottom of the facing so that the lowest set of purl bumps show on the right side. In the first case, you would use mattress stitch, and in the second case you use mattress stitch on the body and whipstitch around the sleeve stitches. Both seams are practically invisible. A third alternative is to use whipstitch for the entire sleeve seam, in which case you'll have a seam that's visible on the right side.

Most knitters will already be familiar with the mattress stitch, and all three of the following seam methods are used in Norwegian knitting. Use the method that gives you the desired look. You may find yourself using one method all the time or switching up and using different seams for different style sweaters.

If you choose to work the mattress/whipstitch method

1. Thread a yarn needle with enough yarn to sew in the sleeve (about three times the distance around the entire opening on the body). Hold the body and sleeves with the right sides out, and the marked center of the sleeve at the shoulder seam; the sleeve facing should be held to the inside of the body, and for now the cut edge of the armhole can face toward the sleeve (it will turn to the inside naturally as the seam is sewn).

2. Insert the needle into the top of the center stitch of the sleeve and into the shoulder seam, and pull the yarn about halfway through. After calculating the ratio of stitches to rows, begin sewing the sleeve into the body. Insert the needle into the next stitch of the sleeve the same way you'd taken the first stitch at the center, and pull the yarn through. Sew into the next stitch in the body, mattress-stitch fashion. Continue sewing in this way to the bottom of the armhole, making sure to skip rows as needed.

3. When you've reached the bottom of the armhole, make the last couple of stitches through the body by sewing vertically. At the center of the underarm, draw the sewing yarn to the inside and you're ready to sew the other side of the armhole. Sew the other side of the armhole in the same way, from the shoulder to the bottom of the armhole,

Sleeve held in place and with first stitch taken.

Working mattress stitch on the body.

Working whipstitch on the sleeve.

Stitching along the bottom of the armhole.

and across the remaining half of the underarm. Draw the end of the sewing yarn to the inside. Secure both ends of the yarn used for the seam.

4. Turn the body and sleeve with the wrong side facing, and neatly trim excess or frayed ends from the cut edges of the armhole, making sure to trim without cutting into the machine stitching. Next, turn the cut edge and facing toward the body, making sure the cut edge is covered. Pin the facing to the body. It's important not to pull or stretch the facing at this point; if you do, the right side will pucker, and there will be a ridge along the armhole on the right side. To prevent this from happening, just use your fingers to smooth the curled edge of the facing down and pin into place.

5. Using the long end of yarn left over after binding off the facing, sew the facing to the body from the underarm, up and around the armhole to the other side. You'll want to sew the seam so that the facing stays in place but make sure the stitches are not tight. By leaving the stitches a little looser, there's wearing ease so the armhole won't bind and there's less likelihood of the seam showing on the right side. Wherever possible, I always like to catch the sewn yarn through a short float, and even split the back of a stitch if sewing with a contrasting yarn color in an area with no floats.

If you choose to use mattress stitch for both parts of the seam, take your stitches in the body as described earlier, and into the sleeve below the facing (see the bottom photo). All the purl bumps are to the inside, and you have a very clean edge.

If you choose to whipstitch the entire seam, prepare the body and sleeves as directed for the mattress/whip seam. Take the first stitch in the same way. Bring the needle back around to the side you took the first stitch and sew into the next stitch and row as before, and then continue down the side of the armhole in the same way (see the photos at the top of next page). The small, diagonal stitches visible on the right side will have a decorative effect, especially when worked over areas of another color.

Pinning the facing in place.

The completed sleeve facing.

Working mattress stitch on the sleeve.

Working whipstitch on both the body and the sleeves.   The finished seam.

FOR SQUARE ARMHOLES

The square armhole doesn't have the cut edge at the bottom to worry about, since the entire width of the armhole was removed at one time while working the body. The sleeve cap fits neatly into the armhole without additional shaping; the sleeve is simply worked back and forth for the height of the sleeve cap after the required length to the underarm has been reached, and the facing was added above the sleeve cap.

Like the drop shoulder sleeve, the circumference at the top of the sleeve for a square armhole needs to be twice the depth of the armhole. Unlike the drop shoulder sleeve, this sleeve doesn't need the extra few stitches to go around the bottom of the armhole; the height of the sleeve cap will fit into the bottom of the opening. So, when making the facing at the top of the sleeve for a square armhole, a few rows (usually five or six, depending on the pattern and yarn) of reverse stockinette are worked without increasing at each end.

Sewing in the sleeves for square armholes is similar to sewing in a drop shoulder sleeve.

1. Begin at the center of the sleeve and shoulder seam, and work down each side of the armhole.
2. When you reach the bound-off stitches at the bottom of the armhole, sew the side edges of the sleeve cap to the bound-off stitches at the bottom of the opening.
3. Trim the cut edges of the armhole, and pin the facing over the top of the cut edge in the same way as for drop shoulder armholes. You can use the long tail left from binding off the sleeve to sew the facing to the body.

FOR SHAPED ARMHOLES

Although shaped armholes and sleeve caps are not typically found on traditional Norwegian sweaters, modern interpretations do occasionally use them. Cutting stitches added at the armholes make following colorwork patterns easy as the knitter shapes the armhole. Modern knitters will be familiar with the basic construction of sleeves for these armholes; worked in the round to the underarm, the cap is then shaped by working it back and forth in rows. Because the pattern will continue up into the sleeve cap, take care to ensure proper gauge or the fit across the shoulders into the upper arms will be tight.

Because there is more involved shaping for the sleeve cap, a knitted facing is not normally worked along the top edges of this sleeve. Instead, the facing is added after the sleeve has been sewn into the armhole. The sleeve is usually sewn in using a backstitch or mattress stitch with a seam allowance of one stitch on the sleeve's vertical edges and one row along the horizontal edges.

1. Hold the sweater with the wrong side out. The armhole should be in front of you so that you can look down into it and you are looking at the right (knit) side of the cut edge. (The sleeve can be left inside when making this facing.) Begin at the right end of the cut edge and pick up stitches along the entire cut edge, holding the cut edge vertical and working from front to back, *through one layer only*, between the machine stitching and the sleeve seam. Use the size needle for normal stockinette knitting to pick up stitches for your stitch gauge.

2. Work a few rows of stockinette so that the purl side of the facing will be next to the purl side of the body. The knit side will be visible on the inside when complete. Since there was some armhole shaping worked at the lowest end of the cutting stitches, make sure to increase a stitch every other row where the straight edge of the armhole begins to curve toward the side of the body so that the facing will lie flat.

3. Bind off, leaving a long tail to use for sewing the facing to the body.

4. Trim the cut edges, being careful not to cut the machine stitching. Fold the facing toward the body and cover the cut edges, and then sew the facing to the body in the same way as for drop shoulder armholes.

The sleeve being sewn into the armhole.

Picking up stitches using the crochet hook method.

Working the facing.

The finished seam.

BRAID AND RIBBON FACINGS

A woven braid or ribbon can also be used to face cut edges. Twill tape or grosgrain ribbon work well for seams done on the inside of garments. For faced seams showing on the right side, think about using a traditional or fashion ribbon. Take into consideration, though, the type of armhole your sweater has. Most braids and ribbons can be used for straight edges only and will need to be mitered to turn any corners.

Braids used for facings should be at least ³/₄" (2cm) wide to look best and still cover cut edges neatly. Wider braids will work on most adult and larger children's sizes (see the Daylily Cardigan on page 150), while baby items and smaller children's sizes should use narrower braids.

Eliminate any facing knitted at the top of the sleeves for this style of facing. Machine-stitch around the armhole like the other styles of armholes, and then cut open.

Pinning the braid to the body.

1. After sewing the shoulder seams, pin the sleeve into the armhole with the cut edge to the side where you'll be attaching the braid or ribbon. Sew the sleeves neatly to the body. A neatly executed backstitch works well here for sleeves with a facing on the right side, but be sure to work it with the sleeve facing you as you sew so that any hand stitching visible after applying the braid is neat and even.

2. Trim the cut edge and turn it toward the body and away from the armhole. Pin the braid over the top of the seam, with one edge next to the hand-sewn seam. Miter the braid to turn the corners at the bottom of the armhole, and fold under the ends of the braid where they meet at the center of the underarm.

Mitering the corners.

3. Neatly sew the braid in place along both edges, and the ends together where they meet at the underarm.

Handle this type of facing in the same way if you're using it on the inside of a garment. This facing can be very useful when working with a heavier yarn, as used for the Cotton Jeans Henley on page 127.

Turning under the ends at the bottom of the armhole.

PART III
Cut Without Fear

CHAPTER 13

Measure, Mark, and Sew

Before you get to cutting your work—the truly scary part (at least the first time)—you'll need to mark the body for the armholes and any front or neck openings. Careful preparation at this stage helps to ensure success, so fear not! If you already sew or do alterations, you will see the parallel steps.

If you're unsure of the holding power of just two sets of machine stitching for any of the openings, sew another line or two of machine stitching. It will all be hidden in the seams and facings. The first step is to feel secure about cutting into your hand-knitted fabric!

MEASURING THE SLEEVES

When making a classic drop shoulder-style sweater, the armhole depth is determined by the width at the top of the sleeve. It's a good idea to check the width on both sleeves. Since knitting tension can (and probably will) vary from the first to the second sleeve, they most likely will not be quite the same width. If there's a great deal of difference in the widths of the two sleeves, it would be wise to rework one of them (if not the entire sleeve, at least a portion of it so that the top width is close to that of the other sleeve). Some adjustment can be made when sewing in the sleeve, but if there's a noticeable difference in widths, it *will* be obvious!

Sweaters with square or shaped armholes won't need to have the armhole depth marked because you'll have already bound off some stitches for the bottom of the armhole, and will only need to mark the center of the cutting stitches.

Before measuring the sleeves, you'll need to mark both sides of the body for the left and right sides of the body; this is where the side markers had been placed while knitting. Thread a needle with contrasting scrap yarn and run a line of basting or running stitches down that line between stitches, or down the center of the stitch if a *fake seam stitch* was used as in the Svale Pullover. The basting should extend from the top edge to below where the bottom of the armhole should be. Make sure the basting yarn is clearly visible on the outside.

Lay the sleeve flat and place a tape measure along the top edge directly below the facing. Make a note of the measurement and then subtract about 1/4" (.6cm) so that the underarm edge of the sleeve will fit around the bottom of the armhole. Keep in mind that the amount subtracted from the width of the sleeve can vary, depending on the gauge of your work.

Marking the side of the body with contrast yarn.

Measuring the width of sleeve.

MARKING THE BODY

THE ARMHOLE

Once you have the sleeve measurement, you can mark it on the side of the body of your sweater. For shoulders that have a row of reverse stockinette before the bind-off, measure from the center of that line created by the reverse stockinette (one purl bump should be above, and one below where you begin measuring). If you'll be joining the shoulders by binding off the shoulder stitches together, mark from the bottom of the live stitches (or the bound-off edge of the armhole cutting stitches). Place a pin, or run a couple of basting stitches at the marked length, perpendicular to the marked opening.

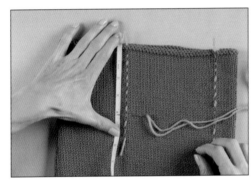

Marking the armhole depth on the body.

CUTTING STITCHES

At this time, you'll also want to use contrasting scrap yarn to mark the center of the cutting stitches for the front opening of cardigans and vests, as well as the center of cutting stitches for zipper openings, and V-necks or crewnecks that have been worked in the round. Centers of cutting stitches for shaped armholes should also be marked in the same way; the bottom of the armhole was the opening created by binding off stitches, so just the center of the cutting stitches needs to be marked with contrasting yarn.

It may also be helpful to mark both sides of the cutting stitches as a guide for your machine stitching.

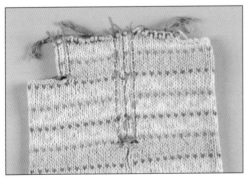

Sides of cutting stitches marked with a second contrasting yarn.

NECKLINES

Necklines that need to be sewn and cut should be marked as well. Find the center of both the front and back of the body and mark each one. Using the neck width stated in the pattern (either as a measurement or a number of stitches), measure or count out from each center marker and place a marker for the sides of the neck opening; check to make sure each shoulder edge on both the front and back have the same number of stitches, and there are the same number of stitches on each side from the center for the neck width. Place markers for the pattern's front and back neck depths.

Mark the shape of the sew-and-cut neck edge by basting from one side of the neck to the bottom of the neck opening at the center, and then back up to the shoulder on the opposite side of the neck. Most of the neck shaping should be in the lower portion of the neck. The sides should smoothly curve up toward the shoulders.

Neck width and depth marked.

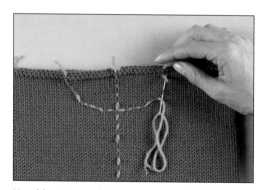

Hand-basting neck shape.

MACHINE STITCHING ARMHOLES

Machine stitching is normally done without any backing added to the piece being sewn because the feed dogs on a sewing machine usually don't snag the back of the sweater. (If you are unfamiliar with sewing machines, these are the ridged pieces that move under the pressure foot while sewing to *feed* the fabric through the machine.)

Even though there isn't a need to use a backing when machine stitching, you may choose to use one if you have numerous long floats on the wrong side of your work or if you're using a particularly delicate yarn. Tear-away interfacings work well, are easy to use, and come in a variety of types. Although iron-on and self-adhesive interfacing are readily available, I would not recommend using them for this purpose. Ironing an interfacing could easily ruin a knitted piece, and self-adhesive products need more surface area to adhere to than a hand-knitted item can provide. If you don't have tear-away interfacing handy, tissue paper will work just as well.

First, cut a strip of the interfacing about 2" (5cm) or more wider than the width of the area to be stitched, and carefully pin it in place. If you'd like, hand-baste it to the wrong side. Once the machine stitching is complete, this interfacing is easily removed and will not leave behind any additional bulk or stiffness.

After you've prepared your sweater pieces for machine stitching, set up the sewing machine as follows:

1. Thread the sewing machine with a contrasting color of sewing thread; you want to be able to see where the stitching is while cutting the opening, as well as when sewing in the sleeves and picking up stitches. The machine stitching will be hidden after the finishing is done, so there's no need to worry about a color that is highly visible!

2. If the machine you're using has an adjustment to remove all pressure from the pressure foot, release the pressure. (This isn't the same as lowering the feed dogs. By lowering the feed dogs, the pressure foot is still pressing down on the work.) If the machine doesn't have such an adjustment, just remember to gently *push* the fabric through the machine—*never* pull it through, or you'll end up with stretched edges that won't steam back into shape.

3. Set the machine to a relatively short stitch length—about 12–14 stitches per 1" (2.5cm). Use a straight stitch, narrow zigzag, stretch stitch, or multiple-stitch zigzag stitch.

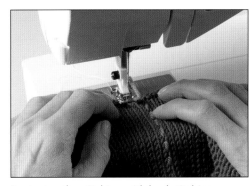
Beginning the stitching with backstitching.

4. Line up the machine needle with the outside edge of the cutting stitches on the left side of the armhole opening; the first line of stitching is done along the outer edges of the cutting stitches, while the second line of stitching is placed inside the area to be cut. Lower the pressure foot and take several stitches. Backstitch several stitches to secure the end of the thread. Carefully sew a straight line to the bottom of the armhole, ending with the needle down in the piece.

5. Lift the pressure foot and turn the work 90° clockwise (to the right) so that you can stitch across the bottom of the opening.

6. Carefully stitch across the four stitches at the bottom of the armhole, ending at the outside edge of the stitch on the other side of the cutting stitches, with the needle down in the piece.

Turning the corner.

7. Turn the work another 90° clockwise so that you can stitch up the other side of the opening. Carefully sew up to the shoulder edge, and backstitch at the edge to secure the thread. Remove the piece from the sewing machine and cut the threads.

8. Sew another line of machine stitching, close to the first line and just inside the cutting stitches. I like to begin the second line of stitching at the side where I just finished the first machine seam, stitch down that side, across the bottom, and then up the other side and end where I'd begun the first machine seam. Place both lines of stitching on top of the legs of the V formed by the stitches. The machine stitching will be visible when I cut into the knitting, pick up stitches, and sew in the sleeves.

The finished stitching with both lines of stitching.

NOTE

I've been asked several times if a serger would work for the machine stitching. Using a serger is not advisable for several reasons: First, turning the corners at the bottom of the armhole would be difficult at best, if not impossible; second, serged stitching is generally not stable enough for this type of application, with the threads pulling out too easily; and third, unless you have a walking foot for your serger, the edge will be stretched out of shape.

MACHINE STITCHING CURVED NECKLINES

The machine stitching around necklines is done in much the same way as for armholes. In most cases, however, the stitching will be done along curved rather than straight lines. There's a greater chance of the piece stretching or twisting out of shape; this would be the perfect time to use tissue paper or tear-away interfacing to help stabilize the piece as you stitch.

Take care when doing the machine stitching so the work doesn't stretch or twist unnecessarily, and follow as smooth a line as possible. A light touch on the machine's pedal is important. Reduce the sewing speed of the machine with a switch or button on the machine itself, if possible.

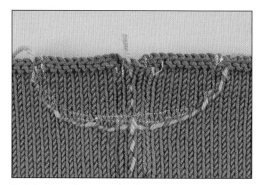

Finished machine stitched neck shape.

MACHINE STITCHING FRONT AND PLACKET OPENINGS

Unless added to existing garments or after the main part of the knitting has been completed, front openings of V-necklines and zipper or button plackets that reach only partway down the body of a sweater are handled a bit differently than armholes. Cardigan and vest fronts are always handled as directed here.

Most openings that extend only partway down the body of a sweater—as will be the case for V-neck pullovers, zip plackets, and buttoned Henley styles—will have from three to five stitches bound off for the bottom of the opening and cutting stitches added so that work can continue in the round. For these types of openings, the machine stitching is done along the sides of the opening only; there's no need to stitch across the bottom of the opening because you'll be cutting through the bottom of the cutting stitches to open the area. Make sure to backstitch at the top and bottom of each line of stitching.

Stitched placket opening.

Stitched V-neck.

Stitched shaped armhole.

Cardigans and vests will typically have their lower bands—whether ribbing or plain stockinette—worked back and forth, and then joined to begin the main part of the body. This reduces bulk at the lower edge under button bands and facings. The machine stitching need not go all the way to the bottom edge or turn row, but only to the bottom of the cutting stitches.

Machine stitching for particularly small cardigans (such as baby sizes) may be more easily done by marking the armholes and front edges, and then stitching the front opening and cutting it open before machine stitching the armholes.

Now that the machine stitching has been done, it's time to get out the scissors.

Stitched cardigan front.

CHAPTER 14

Now for the Cutting (Gasp!)

I f this is the first time you've ever considered cutting into a piece of knitted fabric, you probably fall into one of two polar opposite groups: those who can't wait to forge ahead or those who practically need to be dragged, kicking and screaming, through the process the first time. Whichever group you fall into, or if you're somewhere in between, this is usually the point where even the most fearless knitter needs to pause and take a deep breath before proceeding the first time.

FROM TERROR TO ENTHUSIASM

Although the heading for this section describes my experience with cutting techniques, for most people this technique is generally quick and (relatively) painless. In a multiple-session class I once taught at a yarn shop, one of the participants told me she was ready to do the machine stitching but didn't sew nor did she own a sewing machine. I told her that I'd bring in my machine the next class. The following week, I used the opportunity to show everyone where and how to measure, mark, and sew for the armholes on the sweaters they were making (see chapter 13). I explained that the next step was to sew the shoulders together before sewing in the sleeves. However, before we could do that, I told them (and I was standing there with the sweater in one hand and a pair of scissors in the other) that we would need to cut open the armholes. As I was saying that, I cut open one armhole. From the sharp intake of breath off to my right, I had to turn and make sure we wouldn't have to pick her up off the floor. She recovered from the initial shock and finished the sweater. The next time I taught the class, she brought in a photo; her sweater looked every bit as good as the machine-made versions of the same design that her sisters, also in the photo, were wearing. This was a student, once terrified to cut, who now told me she was "hooked" and couldn't wait to start on another sweater.

TIPS BEFORE CUTTING

If you're still dubious about cutting into the actual sweater, try cutting into the gauge swatch you made beforehand—or at least were supposed to make. Mark a sample armhole on the swatch and machine-stitch around the area. An old sweater that you've been wanting to get rid of for some time also makes a good practice piece; however, using one that's been felted doesn't count.

A good (sharp) pair of scissors or fabric shears is essential; scissors that aren't sharp won't cut cleanly and can make it difficult to cut through all types of yarn. Sharp embroidery scissors work well, too.

As you look at the armhole or placket, the area where you will be cutting is down the center of the opening, through the line marked by the contrast yarn you basted in earlier. You can either cut right through the contrast yarn, completely remove it, and cut down the center of the cutting stitches, or pull it out a few stitches and cut, and then repeat this until getting to the bottom of the opening.

If you pull the yarn out a few stitches at a time, it leaves a sort of "trail" of holes, making it easier to see where you need to cut. This is a handy visual aid, especially if your color pattern makes the stitches hard to distinguish the line on which to cut. To begin

Starting to cut the armhole.

Ending at the bottom of the armhole.

1. Hold the piece to be cut with one hand supporting that portion, making sure that the top and bottom layers are separated. If you prefer to cut with the fabric lying flat, insert a piece of cardboard between the layers to keep them separate, so that you won't accidentally cut where you don't want to. Now, *that* would be truly scary.

2. Cut along the center of the opening, being careful not to cut the machine stitching along the sides of the cutting stitches. **For a cardigan** front opening, or a zipper placket that was begun by binding off a few stitches, you can simply cut all the way through the cast-on at the bottom of the opening. **For armholes,** take care not to cut the machine stitching at the bottom of the armhole, but end just above the machine stitching. As you may have guessed, this is the most important reason for using a contrasting thread for the machine stitching; I find it an excellent opportunity to use up thread from a past sewing project.

Cutting through the bottom of cardigan front.

CHAPTER 15

Nothing Fell Apart; So, What's Next?

You've cut the armholes and any front opening, and nothing disastrous has happened. Stitches haven't suddenly and violently sprung apart, and the pieces haven't collapsed into a tangled pile of yarn. But, you wonder, now what are you supposed to do?

If this is the first time you've ever cut into your knitting, stand back and take a few deep breaths—don't hyperventilate or hold your breath. Take comfort in the knowledge that this process does work. And you've done it!

At this point, the rest of the garment can be sewn together, button bands added, zippers sewn in, and neckband worked (if you're cutting out the neckline, see chapter 16). Much of the finishing is completed in the same way you would for any other knitted garment. If you're changing a pattern or designing your own piece and haven't decided how you want to join the shoulders or what sort of facings to use around the armholes or button bands, now is the time you need to make those decisions.

SHOULDER SEAMS AND HEMS

Join the shoulders by either sewing or binding them off as described in chapter 11; or if you're using a pattern, use the steps in the instructions. Keep in mind that the shoulder for a drop shoulder sweater with long sleeves will need a seam that provides more support than on a sleeveless top. This doesn't mean your seam has to be boring, however. Practical shoulder seams can be attractive, too.

Faced hems on sleeves and body are folded to the wrong side and neatly sewn in place. If the hem of the body gets a drawstring or elastic shock cord, leave an opening in the hem on the side opposite to where the cord will be accessed to adjust the length. Slip the cord into the cord stop and adjust the stop to center it on the length of the cord. Begin at the opening worked into the hem facing, and thread one end of the cord through each side of the hem to the opening on the other side of the body. Secure the ends of the cord together; if you knot the cord, take a few stitches with a needle and thread to ensure the cord won't come untied. Slip the knot between the hem and facing, and then sew the remainder of the hem to the body.

SEWING SLEEVES INTO DROP SHOULDER OR SQUARE ARMHOLES

If your sweater is a drop shoulder pullover or cardigan, or one with square armholes, center the pattern on the sleeves at the shoulder seams and sew them in. Make sure you hold the facing to the inside, and sew into the body one stitch in on the body from the machine stitching. Work through one layer of both body and sleeves; don't fold either edge over and sew through two layers. Trim any loose ends from the cut edges of the armhole, being careful not to cut into the machine stitching. Sew the facing to the wrong side of the garment, paying attention so that you don't stretch the facing when pinning it down.

The one pattern in this book that is an exception to this method is the Blue Sky Wrap. The sleeves for the wrap are sewn in so that the facings and cut edges are on the outside of the body, and the facing are sewn to the right side. More detailed instructions for this method are included in the Blue Sky Wrap pattern on page 160.

FINISHING OF SHAPED ARMHOLES WITH SLEEVES

If you have a sweater with shaped armholes, pin the sleeves into the armholes, centering the pattern at the shoulder seams and keeping the underarm edges aligned. Sew the sleeves into place, making sure the cut edges are turned to the inside and the seam is sewn through the body, one stitch in on the body from the machine stitching. Make sure to sew through one layer of body and sleeve here, as well.

Turn the garment with the wrong side facing out; leaving the sleeve inside the body (right side of the sleeve to the right side of the body) will make working the facing more convenient. Using the same needle size used for the body, begin at the lower end of the armhole on one side and pick up and knit stitches along the cut edges of the armhole, picking up stitches between the machine stitching and the seam joining the sleeve to the body. Pick up the stitches through one layer only; don't fold the edge over to pick up stitches.

Work back and forth, and work the number of rows of stockinette given in the pattern you're using—usually five or six rows—and make sure to work the stockinette so the knit side will show on the inside of the garment. If you want, increase one stitch at each end of every other row twice; if the cut edge will extend beyond the bottom of the facing, this will cover the lower ends of the cut edge without having to fold them. Bind off the facing stitches loosely.

Pull the sleeve through so the wrong side of the sleeve is also facing out. Fold the facing over the cut edges of the armhole, pin it to the body, and cover the cut edges. Sew the facing to the body.

Finished facing partly sewn down to show cut edge underneath.

ARMHOLE BANDS AND FRONT PLACKETS

The armhole bands on vests are worked in a similar fashion as the front button bands of cardigans, so both are covered together here. Either can be worked as a single piece or in two stages.

1. THE DOUBLED BAND

This is probably the simplest type of finish for an armhole or button band. It can be worked in either rib or stockinette, and often includes a turn row (the Bouclé Mohair Cardigan, on page 100, is an example of a simple stockinette band without a turn row). Keep in mind, however, that if rib is doubled for a button band, once buttoned, there will be a great deal of bulk where the bands overlap because the rib adds extra bulk.

Doubled band being sewn down, showing the three layers.

For this reason, when used on the front of a vest or cardigan, clasps are commonly used to close the front of the garment so the bands meet at the center front but don't overlap. A row of reverse stockinette or a picot row is frequently added as a turn row for this type of band. The Falk Cardigan (page 72) and Sonora Tunic (page 89) have this type of band.

For *armholes*, with the right side facing, begin at the center under the armhole. For *front button bands*, with the right side facing, begin at the right end of the opening. Use the smaller needle size listed in the pattern you're making and pick up and knit stitches along the cut edge, one stitch in on the body from the machine stitching (make sure the machine stitching is between where you're picking up stitches and the cut edge. For tips on how to pick up stitches along this type of edge, see chapter 16). Join the stitches for an armhole band to work in the round. Work the button band back and forth (the exception to this would be a band with a color-stranded pattern such as the Ambrosia Vest, on page 104, which is worked in the round).

Work as directed for twice the height of the finished band, and then bind off loosely. Fold the band to the inside along the middle of the band, making sure the cut edge is placed *under* the fold (between layers) and the bound-off edge of the band can be sewn to the back of the pick-up row. Sew the band to the wrong side. For bands worked back and forth, sew the ends closed.

When working the buttonhole band, a set of buttonholes will be worked in the top layer of the band before the turn row, and another matching set of buttonholes worked in the bottom (or facing) layer of the band. Once the band is folded in half, line up the buttonholes before sewing the band to the wrong side, and then sew the buttonholes together so that when buttoned, the buttons will come through to the front of the band; use a buttonhole stitch to sew around the buttonholes not only to sew both layers together but to also reinforce the holes.

2. FACED EDGE WITH MINIMAL WIDTH ON THE RIGHT SIDE

This edging is versatile and can be used either alone for a minimalist look or with another edging, such as a single layer of rib. It was used for the armholes of the Ambrosia Vest (page 104) and neck facing for the Bonsai Shawl (page 174). Usually worked in stockinette, it can be combined with rib, as in the Moss Vest (page 138), Oak Vest (page 122), and Royal Llama Linen Cardigan (page 132). The turn row can be either reverse stockinette or a picot row, depending on what further finishing is to be done. The Zara Cardigan (page 95) was also made this way, along with an extra facing on the back to cover the edges of the zipper tape. A wider band of stockinette can also be knit before doing the turn row.

Working this edging is similar to the doubled band. Use the smaller needle size listed in the pattern you're making and pick up and knit stitches along the cut edge, one stitch in on the body from the machine stitching (make sure the machine stitching is between where you're picking up stitches and the cut edge). For tips on how to pick up stitches along this type of edge, see chapter 16. Join the stitches for an armhole band to work in the round. Work the button band facing back and forth.

When you want a small amount of the band showing on the right side, work one or two rows of stockinette *before* doing the turn row. The facing consists of the usual five or six rows of stockinette, plus another one or two rows to take into account the rows worked before the turn row. Make sure to increase a stitch on each side at the bottom of the armhole facing every other row to add some extra width needed to go around the bottom of the armhole. After binding off loosely, trim any ragged ends from the cut edge and turn the cut edge *toward* the body. Fold the edging along the fold line and cover the cut edge, and then sew the facing to the wrong side of the body.

A turn row can be worked *immediately after* picking up stitches and is commonly a row of reverse stockinette; the armhole bands of the Oak and Moss Vests (pages 122 and 138), as well as the front bands of the Oak Vest and Royal Llama Linen Cardigan (pages 132 and 122), were begun this way.

Knit the facing and increase a stitch on each side of the bottom of the armhole every other row to fit around the bottom of the armhole. After binding off loosely, finish the edge, same as directed above, for a band with one or two rows of stockinette on the right side.

3. MINIMAL-FACED EDGE WITH RIB

Because doing a doubled band in rib can be very bulky, the minimal faced edge is a good alternative when you want to use a ribbed edge.

Take a look at the folded edge of the facing; the row of reverse stockinette leaves a ridge of purl bumps along the outer edge. The bumps that lie along that edge and point outward will be used to pick up the stitches for the rib.

Band with stitches being picked up along purl bumps.

Use the smaller needle size listed in the pattern you're making, and pick up and knit stitches through the outer purl bumps. Join the stitches for an armhole band or neckband to work in the round. Work a button band back and forth. Make the band in rib, or try garter stitch. Bind off in pattern. When the band is buttoned, you'll see how the bulk of the opening has been reduced by spreading most of the bulk (cut edge and facing) away from the center.

4. SINGLE-LAYER RIB WORKED BEFORE THE FACING

Another way of making button bands, as well as armhole edgings, is to work the ribbing first, and then pick up stitches to make the facing. The collar for the Green Line Cabled Pullover (page 109) was done this way.

Once the armhole or front opening has been stitched and cut, hold the piece with the right side facing. Use the smaller needle size listed in the pattern you're using and pick up and knit stitches along the cut edge, one stitch in on the body from the machine stitching (make sure the machine stitching is between where you're picking up stitches and the cut edge. For tips on how to pick up the stitches, see chapter 16). Join the stitches for an armhole band to work in the round. Work the button band facing back and forth.

Work the required length of rib, and then bind off. Hold the piece, again with the right side facing, and fold the rib toward the right side of the body and out of your way, so that the cut edge is again in front of you. Using the same-size needles, pick up the same number of stitches you had for the rib, going through the same spaces as for the rib to pick up this second set of stitches. Work back and forth, or join to work in the round, depending on your pattern.

Knit five or six rows of stockinette for the facing, or the length listed in the pattern instructions; increase one stitch at each end of every other row twice along curved edges. Bind off the facing stitches loosely. Trim any frayed ends from the cut edge, being careful not to cut the machine stitching. Turn both cut edge and facing toward the body so the facing covers the cut edge. Neatly sew the facing to the wrong side.

Rib knit and ready to pick up stitches for facing.

Picking up stitches for the facing.

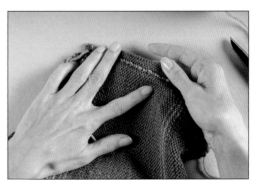

The wrong side of the body after picking up facing stitches.

5. VERTICAL RIB BAND

A cardigan or vest, as well as the vest armhole openings, can also be made with a band of vertical rib. Both the rib and the facing will be worked at the same time, and then sewn into the front opening or armhole.

When used at the front of a cardigan or vest, the lower edge is usually ribbed, and then the stitches for the button bands are placed on holders to be worked later. In this case, slip the stitches from the holder to the smaller-size double-pointed needles used for the rib. Cast on four or five stitches for the facing next to the stitches that will be sewn to the cut edge; work these new stitches in stockinette so that the knit side shows on the inside when the placket and facing have been sewn in place. Make the band the length given in the pattern you're making, and then either bind off all stitches or bind off just the facing stitches for a neckband will be picked up around the entire neck edge.

To attach this band and facing to the body, sew the band through the last rib stitch and on the body, along the cut edge, one stitch in on the body from the machine stitching (make sure the machine stitching is between the cut edge and your seam). Trim any frayed ends from the cut edge, and then fold both the cut edge and facing toward the body so the facing covers the cut edge. Neatly sew the facing to the wrong side.

A band for an armhole would simply be made by casting on all rib and facing stitches at the same time and working for the required length. You can use a provisional cast-on for a less bulky seam at the underarm, and either join the ends using a three-needle bind-off, or graft the ends together with Kitchener stitch. You'll probably need to work a bit more length to this band, or include some short rows to shape the lower ends to ease the facing around the lower part of the armhole.

Sewing in a vertical ribbed band.

The finished band on the wrong side.

PUTTING IN A ZIPPER

There are a couple of options for inserting zippers into a cardigan or pullover. The most basic involves simply folding under the cut edge of the opening so the machine stitching is to the wrong side. Pin the zipper in place and stitch along both sides of the zipper. Whether the zipper is sewn in by hand or machine is your choice, depending on your level of sewing skills. If stitching by machine, take care at the bottom of a closed zipper (for a pullover) to avoid hitting any part of the zipper, or you're likely to break the needle. The other option is to add a placket to the front edges before sewing in the zipper. These plackets are typically very narrow, just three or four rows showing on the right side. Sometimes a simple stripe is worked using some of the colors in the sweater.

Adding a facing behind the zipper is always a nice touch and can help to keep out cold drafts. In the Heilo Pullover (page 116), a piece of machine-knitted rib was supplied with the zipper. You can substitute a plain or decorative braid or ribbon. A separate U-shaped facing was knit for the Moss Vest (page 138).

To add the zipper facing, cut two pieces of facing longer than the zipper tape that are equal lengths. Pin each half of the facing to the back of the zipper so that the right side will show on the inside of the sweater, and the inner edges of the facing meet at the center back of the zipper. Baste the facing in place; you'll now be handling the facing and zipper as one piece, which will make it easier to work with as you sew. The facing can always be added after the zipper is sewn in, and if you're using as decorative braid or ribbon, this may give a cleaner look to the inside of the sweater.

To insert a zipper, pin it into the opening and place the bottom stop at the bottom of the opening. Turn the top ends of the zipper tape down and slightly away from the zipper. This keeps the ends out of the way when you add the neckband, as well as making sure they end up under any facing and won't get caught in the zipper as it's opened and closed. If you don't have a zipper that is the correct length, it's always better to use one that is longer than the opening, rather than shorter. Simply measure the correct length and stitch around the zipper teeth for the new top edge—make sure the zipper slide is below the stitching.

When sewing the zipper in, "stitch in the ditch" (stitch where the placket meets the body). Here, you'll want to use matching sewing thread unless you're after a colorful effect. If the placket at the front opening is very thick, it may tend to roll out and away from the zipper. This can be tamed by sewing the underside of the placket to the zipper tape after the zipper has been sewn in.

Applying a zipper to a cardigan is much the same procedure, though you'll be sewing along one side, and then the other. It will be easier to sew in one side of the zipper before pinning it to the other side of the body. Before you go to pin the second side of the body to the zipper tape, though, make sure the zipper has been closed. This will help you line up the bottom and neck edges of the cardigan or vest.

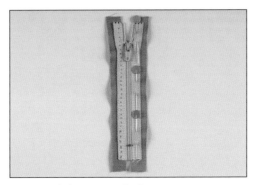

Zipper with facing attached.

Pinning in the zipper.

CHAPTER 16

Do You Need to Cut for a Neckline?

From time to time, a pattern will instruct you to knit straight to the shoulder without doing any neck shaping, or you may simply want to see what the sweater looks like before deciding on a neck shape. One advantage to working the sweater to the shoulder before shaping the neck is that you can continue the color pattern without interrupting the flow of your knitting to figure out where to start each row of the pattern starts while decreasing.

The neck opening will be marked and machine-stitched during the finishing process, as discussed in chapters 10, 13, and 15. Adding the neckband and the actual cutting of the neck opening are covered here in more detail. You have the same options for facing the cut edge as discussed for front plackets in chapter 15; these include the doubled band, and a minimal edging with or without a single layer of rib or garter, or even stockinette. The neck and front opening for the Bouclé Mohair Cardigan (see page 100) was done this way, with a single layer of stockinette above a narrow, faced edge. Simply choose a facing and neckband to complement the rest of the design.

Why Make the Neckband before Cutting?

Unlike button bands and other plackets, the neck opening is usually cut open after picking up and working the neckband. Although the machine stitching stabilizes the knitted fabric of the sweater, there will be unusual stress on the seam if the neck is cut out first.

Working the neckband before you cut also gives you one last out in case you decide you really wanted a V-neck instead of a crewneck, or some other neckline shape. Granted, picking out the machine stitching will not rank as one of your top-ten favorite things to do, but it will allow you to change your mind.

THE NECKBAND

After getting the armholes and neck opening marked and machine-stitched (as described in chapter 13), the armholes cut open, and the shoulder seams joined, you're ready to make the neckband. When joining shoulders using a whipstitched seam, sew only as far as the machine stitching at the neck, and then fasten off. Use the line of contrast yarn basting you set in earlier as the guide for picking up the neckband stitches. Picking up the stitches with a crochet hook (one without a wider handle) will be quicker than trying to knit them up. The crochet hook without a wider handle is used so that as you pick up stitches, you can simply slide them down the shank of the hook and off onto your needles. A crochet hook one size (one-half metric size) smaller than your knitting needles will give you a neat pickup line.

PICKING UP STITCHES

Hold the sweater with the right side facing, the crochet hook in the front, and the yarn at the wrong side. Don't fold the sweater along the machine-stitched line but work through one layer, from right side to wrong side for each stitch (see photo on the right).

Picking up stitches for the neckband on a sewn-and-cut neck opening.

Insert the hook through the single layer of sweater, hold the yarn under the hook and catch the yarn with the hook as if you were knitting, and draw the loop through to the right side. Normally when you crochet, the yarn is wrapped around the top of the hook; if you do this, the stitch will be twisted when you go to transfer it to the needle. By wrapping the yarn under the hook, the stitch will be sitting on the hook properly as you slide it onto the needle, and you won't need to stop and untwist each stitch. Continue picking up stitches until you have about 12 or 15 stitches on the hook, and then slide all of them onto your needle at the same time. Finish picking up all the neckband stitches, and then work the neckband as directed in the pattern instructions. Keep in mind, any ribbing will be extra thick when the cut edge is placed between the layers. So if you're planning a ribbed neck-band, you can reduce bulk by decreasing a few stitches and switching to stockinette after the turn round, or try knitting the neckband in a finer yarn. The Zara Cardigan (see page 95) was done this way.

NOTE

Regarding the number of stitches to pick up along the neck edge: Not all patterns will tell you an exact number of stitches to pick up along a neck, front, or armhole edge. If your pattern doesn't give a number of stitches to be picked up, use the stitch gauge to determine the approximate number, and adjust it for the smaller needle size, and then pick up that number of stitches every 2" (2.5cm) along the edge. This is particularly good to keep in mind when the neckband will be done in a finer yarn.

CUTTING OUT THE NECK SHAPE

Once the neckband is finished, you can trim away the excess fabric from the neck opening. Use sharp scissors to trim alongside the machine stitching, making sure the machine stitching is *between* the neckband and where you're cutting. Take care to not cut the machine stitching or another part of the sweater.

Fold the neckband to the inside and over the cut edge of the neck. Sew the neckband in place. For other options, refer back to chapter 15 for information on the various types of front bands.

Cutting out the excess fabric at the neck.

Fold neckband over cut edge.

PART IV
Patterns

Women's Sweaters

Sizes
XS (S, M, L, XL)
Sample size is Medium

Measurements
Bust: 34 (38, 42, 46, 50)"/86.5
(96.5, 106.5, 117, 127)cm
Body Length: 21¹/₂ (23, 23, 24¹/₂,
24¹/₂)"/54.5 (58.5, 58.5, 62, 62)cm
Sleeve Length: 19¹/₂" (49.5cm) for all sizes

Yarn
Falk by Dale of Norway (100% pure new
    wool, 116 yd. [106m]/1³/₄ oz. [50g])
5 (6, 7, 8, 9) balls, color #5764 Indigo (MC)
2 (3, 3, 4, 4) balls, color #7053 Bottle Green
    (CC1)
3 (3, 4, 4, 5) balls, color #6943 Sea Green
    (CC2)
2 (2, 2, 3, 3) balls, color #9133 Spring
    Green (CC3)
1 (1, 1, 1, 1) ball, color #2642 Sandlewood
    (CC4)
3 (4, 4, 5, 5) balls, color #0083 Charcoal
    Heather (CC5)

Needles and Notions
1 each U.S. size 2 and 3, or 4 (2.75mm and
    3.25mm or 3.5mm) circular needles, or
    size needed to obtain gauge
1 set each U.S. size 2 and 3, or 4 (2.75mm
    and 3.25mm or 3.5mm) double-pointed
    needles, or size needed to obtain gauge
Crochet hook U.S. size 2 or A (1.5mm or
    2mm)
Stitch markers
Blunt tapestry needle
Contrasting sewing thread
7 buttons, ³/₄" (1.9mm)—#0330-0215U
    Kongsberg from Dale of Norway

Gauge
24 sts and 28 rnds over colorwork using
    larger needle = 4" (10cm)

▶ Take time to check your gauge.

Falk Cardigan

DALE DESIGN

This cardigan is a great example of contemporary Norwegian design, incorporating a variety of overall and placed patterns. I couldn't resist adding additional colors to the pattern while leaving the background in a single color. I've altered the finishing of the original pattern by adding a neckband with mitered corners that goes all the way around the neck. Instead of binding off the button bands and simply sewing them down, I grafted the live stitches to the inside along the pickup row. The result gives you a beautifully tailored look. This piece will be easy to customize by choosing your own colors, or adding velvet ribbon to the sleeves, front edges, and neck.

DIRECTIONS
BODY

With smaller circ needle and CC5, CO 191 (227, 245, 263, 299) sts. Working back and forth, beg with a RS row and work 7 rows of St st, then knit 1 row for fold line.

With RS facing, CO 4 new sts at end of row for cutting sts; work cutting sts in St st throughout and do not include in pattern or st counts. Join and, working in the rnd, make sure sts are not twisted. Mark beg of rnd and beg rnds at center of cutting sts.

Place side markers 47 (56, 60, 65, 74) sts out from both sides of cutting sts. Cont St st and work first 7 rnds of Pattern I, beg as shown on chart (page 76), then work 8-st rep to end of rnd. Change to larger circ needle, then complete Pattern I and inc 1 st at center of last rnd—192 (228, 246, 264, 300) sts.

Set pattern across next rnd as follows: Work cutting sts, work Pattern II over next 6 sts, Pattern III over next 180 (216, 234, 252, 288) sts, Pattern IV over next 6 sts, then work rem cutting sts. Cont as est, working colors over Patterns II and IV using same CC as Pattern III, and work 18-rnd rep of Pattern III 5 (5¹/₂, 5¹/₂, 6, 6) times; body should measure approx 18 (19¹/₂, 19¹/₂, 21, 21)"/45.5 (49.5, 49.5, 53.5, 53.5)cm from fold line.

Work Pattern V, ending last rnd 18 (18, 19, 20, 21) sts before end of rnd; body should measure approx 18¹/₂ (20, 20, 21¹/₂, 21¹/₂)"/47 (51, 51, 54.5, 54.5)cm from fold line.

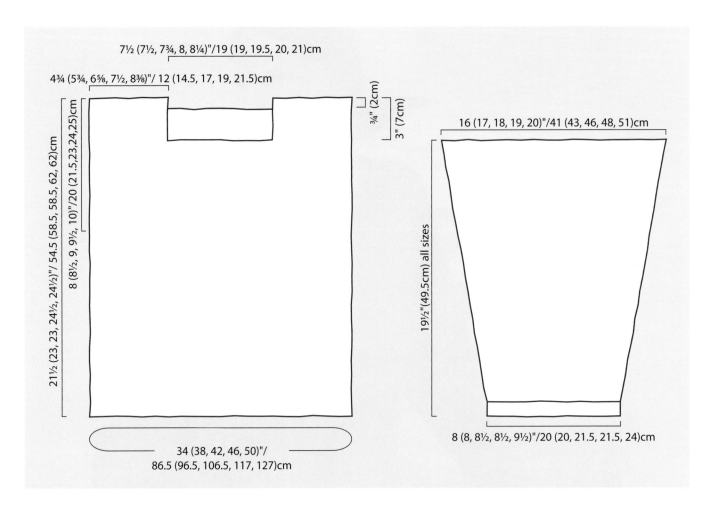

7½ (7½, 7¾, 8, 8¼)"/19 (19, 19.5, 20, 21)cm

4¾ (5¾, 6⅝, 7½, 8⅜)"/ 12 (14.5, 17, 19, 21.5)cm

¾" (2cm)

3" (7cm)

21½ (23, 23, 24½, 24½)"/ 54.5 (58.5, 58.5, 62, 62)cm

8 (8½, 9, 9½, 10)"/20 (21.5,23,24,25)cm

34 (38, 42, 46, 50)"/
86.5 (96.5, 106.5, 117, 127)cm

16 (17, 18, 19, 20)"/41 (43, 46, 48, 51)cm

19½"(49.5cm) all sizes

8 (8, 8½, 8½, 9½)"/20 (20, 21.5, 21.5, 24)cm

FRONT NECK OPENING

Bind off the next 40 (40, 42, 44, 46) sts for front neck opening (the 4 cutting sts, plus 18 [18, 19, 20, 21] sts on either side), change to CC5 and work to end of rnd—156 (192, 208, 224, 258) sts.

CO 4 new cutting sts, then join and, working in the rnd again, cont St st with CC5 until body measures 20¾ (22¼, 22¼, 23¾, 23¾)"/52.5 (56.5, 56.5, 60.5, 60.5)cm from fold line. Work first 4 rnds of Pattern VI.

BACK NECK OPENING

Next rnd, work front sts and first 29 (38, 41, 45, 53) sts of back, bind off the next 40 (40, 44, 44, 46) sts for back

neck opening, then work to end of rnd—116 (152, 164, 180, 212) sts. Cut yarn, then slip cutting sts and left shoulder sts (from both front and back) from right needle to left needle. Reattach yarn and, working back and forth, beg rows at back neck edges. Beg with a RS row and complete pattern.

Knit 1 row on WS (or purl 1 row on RS), then bind off.

SLEEVES

With smaller dpns and CC5, CO 49 (49, 53, 53, 57) sts. Join and, working in the rnd, make sure sts are not twisted. Mark beg of rnd.

Knit 7 rnds. Purl 1 rnd for fold line. Work first 7 rnds of Pattern I, placing center of pattern at center of sleeve.

Change to larger dpns, then complete pattern. **At the same time,** inc 1 st at the beg and end of every 5th rnd 25 (13, 12, 0, 0) times, every 4th rnd 0 (15, 17, 32, 30) times, then every 3rd rnd 0 (0, 0, 0, 3) times, leaving 2 sts between inc sts and working inc sts into pattern.

In the meantime, when Pattern I is complete, beg Pattern VII, placing center of pattern at center of sleeve, and cont inc as est—99 (105, 111, 117, 123) sts. **At the same time,** when sleeve measures approx 17" (43cm) from fold line, end Pattern VII.

Work Pattern V.

Knit 4 rnds with CC5, then work Pattern VI; sleeve should measure approx 19¹/₂" (49.5cm) from fold line.

Purl 5 rnds for facing and, **at the same time,** inc 1 st at the beg and end of 1st rnd, then every other rnd twice more—105 (111, 117, 123, 129) sts. Bind off loosely.

Make second sleeve to match.

FINISHING

Block pieces to finished measurements; wet blocking works well with this yarn.

Measure sleeves for armhole depth and mark on each side of body where side markers have been placed, from purl row at shoulders down for armhole openings.

Sew 2 rows of machine stitching, 2 sts out from both sides of where markers were placed and across bottom of the 4 sts for armholes, and along both sides of cutting sts for front opening. Cut open armholes and front opening.

Sew shoulders tog using whip st through purl row at top of shoulders.

Fold lower edges of body and sleeves to inside along fold lines and sew neatly to WS.

FRONT PLACKETS

With smaller circ needle, CC5 and with RS facing, beg at lower edge of right front and pick up and k12 sts per 2" (5cm) along right front edge to neck edge.

Working back and forth, beg with a WS row and work 5 rows of St st. Purl 1 row on RS for fold line. Work 4 rows of St st.

Fold placket to inside along fold line, covering cut edge, and neatly sew sts to pick up row on WS using Kitchener st. (**Optional:** Bind off sts, then fold placket to inside along fold line and neatly sew facing to WS.) Work placket and facing along rem front edge to match.

NECKBAND

With smaller circ needle, CC5 and with RS facing, pick up sts along neck edge and ends of front plackets in same manner as plackets, making sure to pick up 1 st at each corner of neck edge.

Working back and forth, beg with a WS row and work 5 rows of St st. **At the same time,** dec 2 sts at each corner of neck by working to 1 st before corner st, s2kp for centered double decrease.

Purl 1 row on RS for fold line.

Work 4 rows of St st for facing, making sure to inc 1 st on each side of marked st every RS row by lifting horizontal strand between st just worked and next st, then k tbl.

Fold neckband to inside along fold line and sew to pick up row in same manner as plackets. Neatly sew ends of neckband and lower ends of plackets closed.

Mark placement for buttons along both plackets, placing top button at center of neckband, bottom button approx ³/₄" (2cm) from bottom edge, then evenly space rem buttons in between.

Crochet button loops along right front edge, centering each over a marker. Securely sew buttons to left placket as marked.

Pin sleeves into armholes, with facings to inside, and centers of sleeves at shoulder seams. Sew sleeves to body, working from shoulder down with whip st or combined whip st/mattress st. On inside, turn facings toward body, covering cut edges, then neatly sew facings to WS.

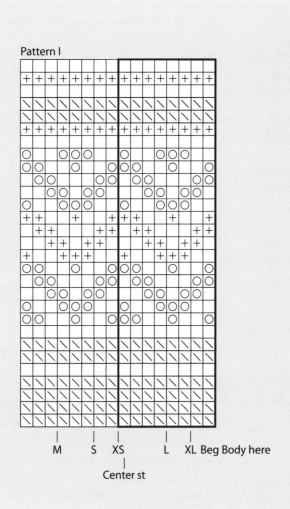

Pattern I

indigo (MC)

charcoal heather (CC5)

bottle green (CC1)

sea green (CC2)

spring green (CC3)

sandlewood (CC4)

Repeat

M   S   XS   L   XL Beg Body here

Center st

Pattern IV

Pattern III

Pattern II

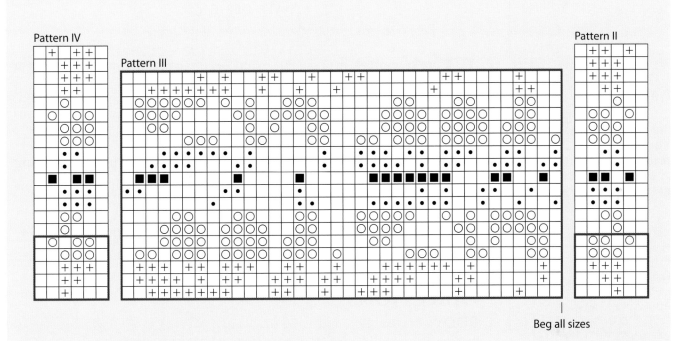

Beg all sizes

Note: Row repeat for both Pattern II and IV are 5 rnds, follow color repeat of Pattern III.

Pattern V

Pattern VI

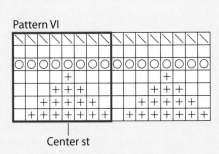

Center st

Pattern VII

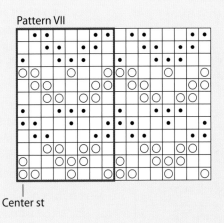

Center st

Svale Pullover

DALE DESIGN

Sizes
XS (S, M, L, XL, XXL)
Sample size is Small

Measurements
Bust: 33 (37, 41, 45, 49, 53)"/84 (94, 104, 114.5, 124.5, 134.5)cm
Body Length: 18¹/₂ (19, 19¹/₂, 20, 20¹/₂, 21)"/47 (48.5, 49.5, 51, 52, 53.5)cm
Sleeve Length: 18³/₄" (47.5cm) for all sizes

Yarn
Svale by Dale of Norway (50% cotton/40% viscose/10% silk, 114 yd. [104m]/1³/₄ oz. [50g])
8 (9, 10, 11, 12, 13) balls, color #2631 Linen (MC)
2 (3, 3, 4, 4, 4) balls, color #5061 Plum (CC1)
2 (2, 2, 2, 3, 3) balls, color #9451 Sage (CC2)
1 (1, 1, 1, 2, 2) ball(s), color #3812 Light Pink (CC3)

Needles and Notions
1 each U.S. size 4 and 5 (3.5mm and 3.75mm) circular needles, or size needed to obtain gauge
1 set each U.S. size 4 and 5 (3.5mm and 3.75mm) double-pointed needles, or size needed to obtain gauge
Crochet hook U.S. size D-3 (3.25mm)
Stitch markers
Stitch holders
Blunt tapestry needle
Contrasting sewing thread

Gauge
22 sts and 28 rnds over St st using larger needles; 23 sts and 28 rnds over color-work pattern using larger needles = 4" (10cm)

➤ Take time to check your gauge.

Here's another wonderful example of contemporary Norwegian sweater design. While the pattern looks amazingly complex, each half of the repeat is really a mirror image of the other half, which actually makes the pattern easier to work and just as easy to memorize.

I tinkered with the original design, slimming the silhouette, deepening the V-neck and adding more eyelet cables. I particularly like the feminine look of the new colors, and think a longer body length, either with or without side shaping, would be equally as successful as the shorter body shown here.

DIRECTIONS
BODY

With smaller circ needle and MC, CO 168 (188, 208, 232, 252, 276) sts. Join and, working in the rnd, make sure sts are not twisted. Mark beg of rnd and knit 5 rnds. Work 1 picot rnd for fold line (*yo, k2tog; rep from * to end of rnd).

Knit 1 rnd and place side markers at the beg of rnd and after 84 (94, 104, 116, 126, 138) sts. Set pattern across next rnd in this manner: P1 st, beg Pattern I as shown on chart (page 82) and work to side marker, p1 st, then beg again on chart at side marker as before, then work to end of rnd. Work 4 more rnds in this manner, working p st after both markers in background color throughout; if only one color is used in a rnd, use that color.

Change to larger circ needle and complete pattern. **At the same time,** inc 1 st on each side of both markers every 16th (12th, 12th, 16th, 12th, 16th) rnd 4 (5, 5, 4, 5, 4) times, leaving p st between inc sts and working inc sts into pattern—184 (208, 228, 248, 272, 292) sts. In the meantime, when pattern is complete, knit 4 rnds with MC; body should measure approx 8" (20.5cm) from fold line.

Next rnd, beg Cable Pattern at marked sts on Pattern I rep, working cable only if all 5 sts can be worked, and work sts between cables in St st; make sure to cont to p first st after each marker. Cont as est until body measures 9¹/₄ (9¹/₂, 10, 10¹/₄, 10³/₄, 11)"/23.5 (25, 25.5, 26, 27.5, 28)cm from fold line.

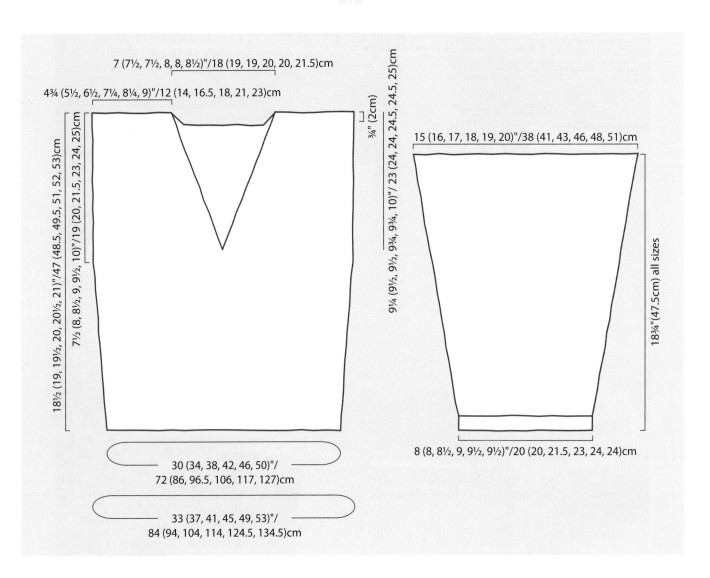

7 (7½, 7½, 8, 8, 8½)"/18 (19, 19, 20, 20, 21.5)cm

4¾ (5½, 6¼, 7¼, 8¼, 9)"/12 (14, 16.5, 18, 21, 23)cm

¾" (2cm)

9¼ (9½, 9½, 9¾, 9¾, 10)"/ 23 (24, 24, 24.5, 24.5, 25)cm

18½ (19, 19½, 20, 20½, 21)"/47 (48.5, 49.5, 51, 52, 53)cm

7½ (8, 8½, 9, 9½, 10)"/19 (20, 21.5, 23, 24, 25)cm

30 (34, 38, 42, 46, 50)"/
72 (86, 96.5, 106, 117, 127)cm

33 (37, 41, 45, 49, 53)"/
84 (94, 104, 114, 124.5, 134.5)cm

15 (16, 17, 18, 19, 20)"/38 (41, 43, 46, 48, 51)cm

18¾"(47.5cm) all sizes

8 (8, 8½, 9, 9½, 9½)"/20 (20, 21.5, 23, 24, 24)cm

FRONT NECK OPENING

Mark center front st (do not include p st after side markers).

Next rnd, work to marked st, bind off 1 st to beg V-neck shaping, then work to end of rnd. Next rnd, cont pattern, any rem side shaping and CO 3 new sts over bound-off st of previous rnd (these are cutting sts; work in St st throughout and exclude from st counts).

Dec 1 st, 1 st in from cutting sts, on each side of front neck opening, every other rnd 0 (0, 0, 7, 7, 8) times, then every 3rd rnd 18 (20, 20, 15, 15, 15) times—147 (167, 187, 203, 227, 245) sts. Work even until body measures approx 17¾ (18¼, 18¾, 19¼, 19¾, 20¼)"/45 (46.5, 47.5, 49, 50, 51.5)cm from fold line, ending with a rnd 3 or 7 of Cable Pattern rep.

BACK NECK OPENING

Next rnd, cont pattern and work front sts, p st after side marker, then work first 32 (36, 41, 44, 50, 54) sts of back, bind off the next 27 (31, 31, 35, 35, 37) sts for back neck opening, then work to end of rnd—120 (136, 156, 168, 192, 208) sts.

Cut yarn and slip left front shoulder sts from right needle to left needle. Reattach yarn and, working back and forth, beg rows at back neck edges and beg with a RS row. Cont pattern and bind off 3 sts at the beg of first 2 rows, then 2 sts at the beg of next 2 rows—110 (126, 146, 158, 182, 198) sts; body should measure approx 18$\frac{1}{2}$ (19, 19$\frac{1}{2}$, 20, 20$\frac{1}{2}$, 21)"/47 (48.5, 49.5, 51, 52, 53.5)cm from fold line.

Next row, work 25 (29, 34, 37, 43, 47) sts, bind off the next 5 sts at side of body (make sure p st is at center of the 5 sts bound off), work next 25 (29, 34, 37, 43, 47) sts, bind off the 3 cutting sts for front neck opening, work next 25 (29, 34, 37, 43, 47) sts, bind off the next 5 sts at side of body as before, then work to end of row. Slip rem 25 (29, 34, 37, 43, 47) sts of each shoulder to st holders.

SLEEVES

With smaller dpns and MC, CO 46 (46, 48, 52, 54, 54) sts. Join and, working in the rnd, make sure sts are not twisted. Mark beg of rnd and knit 5 rnds. Work 1 picot rnd as before for fold line.

Knit 1 rnd and p last st of rnd. Work first 5 rnds of Pattern I, excluding p st at end of rnd from pattern, and beg each size as shown on chart.

Change to larger dpns. Cont pattern and, **at the same time,** inc 1 st at the beg and end of every 7th rnd 9 (0, 0, 0, 0, 0) times, every 6th rnd 9 (15, 10, 0, 0, 0) times, every 5th rnd 0 (6, 10, 24, 20, 8) times, then every 4th rnd 0 (0, 3, 0, 5, 20) times, leaving p st at end of rnd between inc sts and working inc sts into pattern—82 (88, 94, 100, 104, 110) sts.

In the meantime, when Pattern I is complete, knit 4 rnds with MC. Cont St st with MC and work Cable Pattern

over 5 sts as marked on Pattern I rep of chart, and cont rem inc as est.

Work even until sleeve measures 17$\frac{1}{4}$" (44cm) from fold line, ending with a rnd 3 or 7 of Cable Pattern rep.

Work Pattern II, placing center of pattern at center of rnd and cont any rem inc. When pattern is complete, sleeve should measure approx 18$\frac{3}{4}$" (47.5cm) from fold line.

Purl 5 rnds for facing and, **at the same time,** inc 1 st at the beg and end of 1st rnd, then every other rnd twice more—88 (94, 100, 106, 110, 116) sts. Bind off loosely pwise.

Make second sleeve to match.

FINISHING

Block pieces to finished measurements. Fold lower edges of body and sleeves to inside along fold lines and sew neatly to WS.

Measure sleeves for armhole depth and mark on each side of body, from last row down for armhole openings.

Sew 2 rows of machine stitching, 2 sts out from both sides of p st at each side of body and across bottom of the 5 sts for armholes. Sew 2 rows of machine stitching along each side of cutting sts for front neck opening. Cut open armholes and front neck opening.

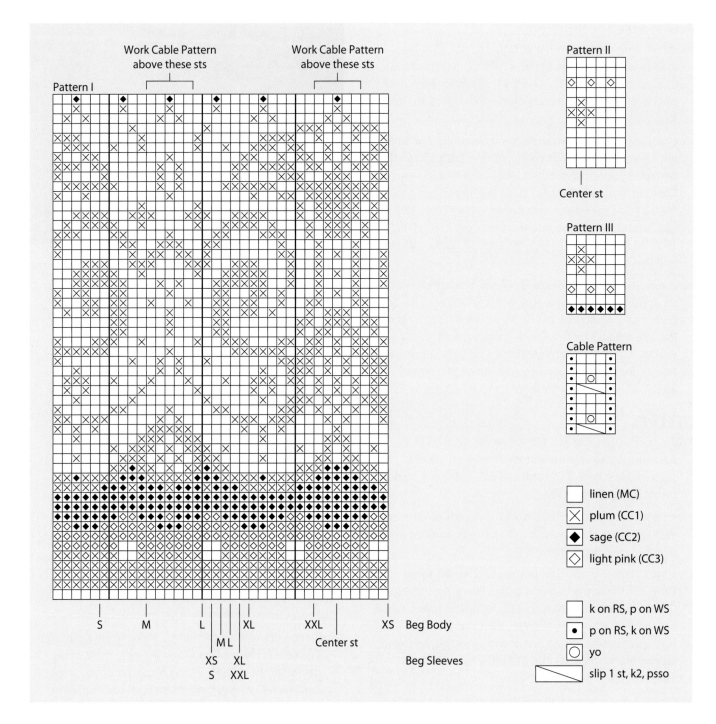

Pattern I

Work Cable Pattern above these sts

Work Cable Pattern above these sts

Pattern II

Center st

Pattern III

Cable Pattern

S   M   L   XL   XXL   XS   Beg Body

M L

Center st

XS   XL

S   XXL   Beg Sleeves

☐   linen (MC)

☒   plum (CC1)

◆   sage (CC2)

◇   light pink (CC3)

☐   k on RS, p on WS

•   p on RS, k on WS

◯   yo

╱   slip 1 st, k2, psso

Holding one side of front and back with WS tog, slip sts for both shoulders to one needle, alternating 1 st from back, 1 st from front.

Bind Off Shoulders

*Lift second st on left needle over first st and off needle, knit the first st and leave on right needle. Rep from * once more—2 sts on right needle. Lift first st worked over second st—1 st left on right needle. Cont working in this way until all sts have been bound off. Rep with rem shoulder.

Neckband

With smaller circ needle, MC and with RS facing, beg at left shoulder and pick up and k11 sts per 2" (5cm) along neck edge, making sure to pick up 1 st at bottom of V-neck at center front (total number of sts picked up should be divisible by 6 + 1).

Join and, working in the rnd, mark beg of rnd. Work Pattern III and, **at the same time,** dec 1 st on each side of st at bottom of V-neck every rnd. When pattern is complete, purl 1 rnd with MC for fold line. Knit 7 rnds, then bind off loosely.

Fold neckband to inside along fold line, covering cut edges, then neatly sew neckband to WS.

Pin sleeves into armholes, with facings to inside, and centers of sleeves at shoulder seams. Sew sleeves to body, working from shoulder down with whip st or combined whip st/mattress st. On inside, turn facings toward body, covering cut edges, then neatly sew facings to WS.

Cruise Boatneck Pullover

Sizes
XS (S, M, L, XL, XXL)
Sample size is Small

Measurements
Bust: 32 (36, 40, 44, 48, 52)"/81.5 (91.5,
   101.5, 112, 122, 132)cm
Body Length: 20¹/₂ (21, 21¹/₂, 22, 22¹/₂,
   23¹/₂)"/52 (53.5, 54.5, 56, 57, 59.5)cm
Sleeve Length: 14¹/₄ (14¹/₄, 13³/₄, 13¹/₄,
   13¹/₄, 13¹/₄)" /36 (36, 35, 33.5, 33.5, 33.5)cm

Yarn
Twinkle Cruise by Classic Elite Yarns (70%
   silk/30% cotton, 120 yd. [110m]/1³/₄ oz.
   [50g])
7 (8, 9, 10, 11, 13) balls, color #66 River

Needles and Notions
1 each U.S. size 3 and 4 (3.25mm and
   3.5mm) circular needles, or size needed
   to obtain gauge
1 set each U.S. size 3 and 4 (3.25mm and
   3.5mm) double-pointed needles, or size
   needed to obtain gauge
Stitch markers
Contrasting sewing thread

Gauge
24 sts and 33 rnds over St st using larger
   needles = 4" (10cm)

   ▸ Take time to check your gauge.

Even simple knit-and-purl patterns are easier to work in the round as this relaxed pullover demonstrates. The short, straight body with ³/₄-length sleeves in a silk/cotton blend yarn show how the sewing and cutting finishing methods can work just as successfully with nontraditional designs. Facings worked at the top edges give the neck and shoulders needed stability.

DIRECTIONS
BODY
With smaller circ needle, CO 188 (208, 236, 256, 280, 304) sts. Join and, working in the rnd, make sure sts are not twisted. Mark beg of rnd.

*Purl 1 rnd, knit 1 rnd; rep from * once more, then purl 1 rnd.

Change to larger circ needle. Knit 1 rnd and inc 4 (6, 4, 8, 8, 8) sts evenly spaced across rnd—192 (214, 240, 264, 288, 312) sts. Place side markers at the beg of rnd and after 96 (107, 120, 132, 144, 156) sts.

Next rnd, *p1, k95 (106, 119, 131, 143, 155) sts; rep from * once more. Work as est until body measures 16¹/₂ (17, 17¹/₂, 18, 18¹/₂, 19¹/₂)"/42 (43, 44.5, 45.5, 47, 49.5)cm from bottom edge.

Purl 1 rnd, knit 1 rnd, then purl 1 rnd. Knit 2 rnds and inc 8 (10, 12, 12, 12, 12) sts evenly spaced across 2nd rnd—200 (224, 252, 276, 300, 324) sts.

Work Pattern A, beg each size as shown on chart and work to marker, then beg again as before and work to end of rnd. Dec 2 sts evenly spaced on rnd 11—198 (222, 250, 274, 298, 322) sts.

When pattern is complete, purl 1 rnd and dec 6 (8, 10, 10, 10, 10) sts evenly spaced across rnd—192 (214, 240, 264, 288, 312) sts. Knit 1 rnd, purl 1 rnd, then knit 1 rnd and end last rnd 5 sts before end of rnd.

FACING
Bind off the next 11 sts for top of armhole, purl next 85 (96, 109, 121, 133, 145) sts for fold line, bind off the next 11 sts for top of armhole, then purl to end of rnd. Working front and back separately, work 5 rows of St st, then bind off neatly.

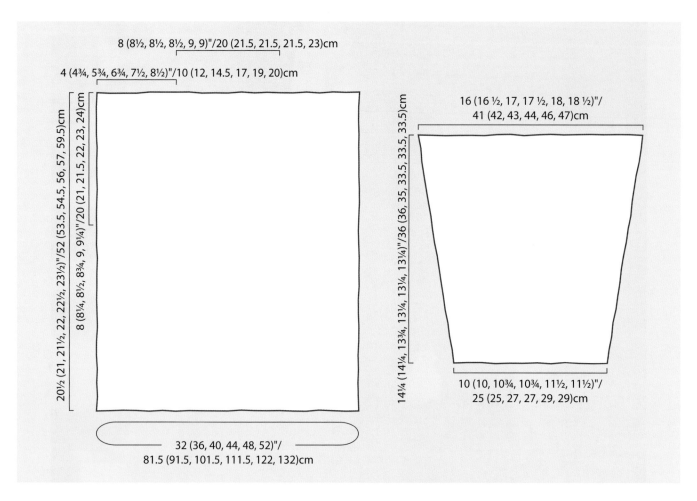

8 (8½, 8½, 8½, 9, 9)"/20 (21.5, 21.5, 21.5, 23)cm

4 (4¾, 5¾, 6¾, 7½, 8½)"/10 (12, 14.5, 17, 19, 20)cm

20½ (21, 21½, 22, 22½, 23½)"/52 (53.5, 54.5, 56, 57, 59.5)cm

8 (8¼, 8½, 8¾, 9, 9¼)"/20 (21, 21.5, 22, 23, 24)cm

32 (36, 40, 44, 48, 52)"/
81.5 (91.5, 101.5, 111.5, 122, 132)cm

16 (16 ½, 17, 17 ½, 18, 18 ½)"/
41 (42, 43, 44, 46, 47)cm

14¼ (14¼, 13¾, 13¼, 13¼, 13¼)"/36 (36, 35, 33.5, 33.5, 33.5)cm

10 (10, 10¾, 10¾, 11½, 11½)"/
25 (25, 27, 27, 29, 29)cm

SLEEVES

With smaller dpns, CO 61 (61, 65, 65, 69, 69) sts. Join and, working in the rnd, make sure sts are not twisted. Mark beg of rnd.

*Purl 1 rnd, knit 1 rnd; rep from * twice more, then knit 1 rnd.

Change to larger dpns. Working last st of every rnd in reverse St st (purl every rnd), work Pattern C over rem sts, placing center of pattern at center of sleeve. **At the same time,** inc 1 st at the beg and end of every 6th rnd 12 (8, 6, 5, 3, 0) times, then every 4th rnd 8 (14, 16, 18, 20, 24) times, leaving p st between inc sts and working inc sts into pattern—101 (105, 109, 111, 115, 117) sts.

When Pattern C is complete, cont to purl last st, and work St st over rem sts. Cont inc as est and work until sleeve measures 12¾ (12¾, 12¼, 11¾, 11¾, 11¾)"/32.5 (32.5, 31, 30, 30, 30)cm from bottom edge.

Cont to purl last st, and rem inc as est, and work Pattern B, placing center of pattern at center of sleeve.

When pattern is complete, knit 3 rnds. Purl 5 rnds for facing and, **at the same time,** inc 1 st at the beg and end of 1st rnd, then every other rnd twice more—107 (111, 115, 117, 121, 123) sts. Bind off loosely.

Make second sleeve to match.

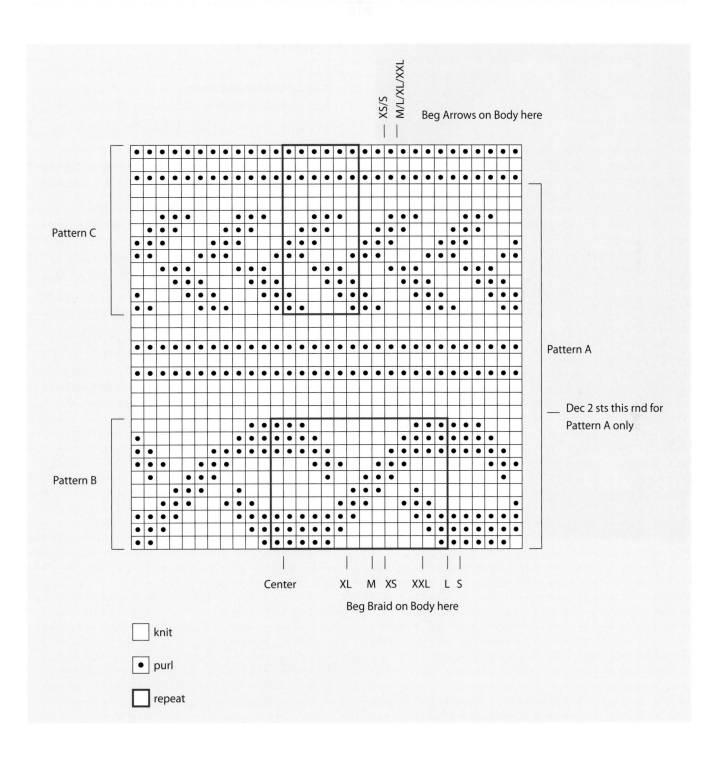

Pattern C

Pattern A

Pattern B

XS/S
M/L/XL/XXL
Beg Arrows on Body here

Dec 2 sts this rnd for
Pattern A only

Center   XL   M XS   XXL   L S

Beg Braid on Body here

□ knit

● purl

□ repeat

FINISHING

Block pieces to finished measurements. *Optional:* Pieces may be wet-blocked if needed.

Measure sleeves for armhole depth and mark on each side of the body, from fold line at shoulders down for armhole openings.

Sew 2 rows of machine stitching, 2 sts out from both sides of purl sts and across bottom of the 5 sts for armholes. Cut open the armholes.

Fold facings at top of shoulders to inside along fold lines and pin to WS. Place markers 4 (4$\frac{1}{4}$, 4$\frac{1}{4}$, 4$\frac{1}{4}$, 4$\frac{1}{2}$, 4$\frac{1}{2}$)"/10 (11, 11, 11, 11.5, 11.5)cm out from center of both front and back along shoulder fold lines for neck opening. Sew shoulders tog using whip st through fold line, beg at armhole stitching and working toward neck.

Pin sleeves into armholes, with facings to inside, and centers of sleeves at shoulder seams. Sew sleeves to body, working from shoulder down with whip st or combined whip/mattress st. On inside, turn facings toward body, covering cut edges, then neatly sew facings to WS. Neatly sew shoulder/neck facings to WS.

Sonora Tunic

Long sweaters and tunics are ideal for knitting in the round but if parts of the sweater need to be worked separately for more than just a few rows, the weight of the piece can stretch those sections out of shape. In order to prevent that from happening here, cutting stitches have been added after binding off stitches at the bottom of the back placket so that most of the body can be worked in the round.

DIRECTIONS

NOTE

When working shaping at back neck and armhole edges, if a yo cannot be worked with its accompanying ssk or k2tog, work those stitches in St st.

BODY

With circ needle, CO 154 (173, 190, 209, 245, 262) sts. Working back and forth, knit 1 row but do not turn. Join and, working in the rnd, make sure sts are not twisted. Mark beg of rnd and beg rnds at center back.

Purl 1 rnd, then knit 1 rnd. Set pattern across next rnd in this manner: p4 (5, 4, 5, 5, 4) sts, beg at right-hand side of chart (page 93) and work first 9 sts, work 18-st rep over next 126 (144, 162, 180, 216, 234) sts, work last 10 sts of chart, then p5 sts.

Cont 44-rnd rep until body measures 10 (10, 10, 10½, 10½, 10½)"/25.5 (25.5, 25.5, 26.5, 26.5, 26.5)cm from bottom edge, ending last rnd 5 sts before end of rnd.

PLACKET OPENING

Bind off 9 (10, 9, 9, 10, 9) sts for placket opening, then work to end of rnd—145 (163, 181, 200, 235, 253) sts. Next rnd, CO 4 new sts, then join and cont working in the rnd (these are cutting sts; work in St st every rnd and exclude from st counts).

Place side markers 34 (38, 43, 48, 57, 61) sts out from both sides of cutting sts, with 77 (87, 95, 104, 121, 131) sts between markers for front. Work even until body measures 19½ (20, 20, 20½, 20½, 21)"/49.5 (51, 51, 52, 52, 53.5)cm from bottom edge and ending with an odd number rnd of rep, and end last rnd before cutting sts.

Sizes
XXS (XS, S, M, L, XL)
Sample size is Small

Measurements
Bust: 30¾ (34½, 38, 41¾, 49, 52½)"/78 (88, 96.5, 106, 124.5, 133.5)cm
Body Length: 27 (27½, 28, 28½, 29, 29½)"/68.5 (70, 71, 72.5, 73.5, 75)cm
Sleeve Length to Underarm: 10 (10½, 10½, 11, 11, 11½)"/25.5 (26.5, 26.5, 28, 28, 29)cm

Yarn
Sonora by Nashua Handknits (46% silk/31% viscose/20% linen/3% nylon, 103 yd. [95m]/1¾ oz. [50g])
9 (10, 11, 12, 14, 15) balls, color #7793 Natural

Needles and Notions
1 U.S. size 7 (4.5mm) circular needle, or size needed to obtain gauge
1 set U.S. size 7 (4.5mm) double-pointed needles, or size needed to obtain gauge
Crochet hook U.S. size G-6 (4mm)—optional
Stitch markers
Stitch holders
Contrasting sewing thread

Gauge
20 sts and 33 rows over pattern = 4" (10cm)

➤ Take time to check your gauge.

Sonora Tunic

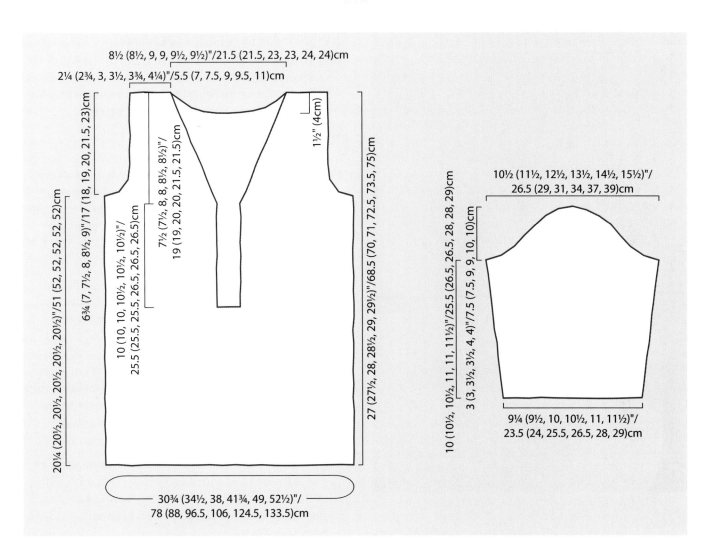

8½ (8½, 9, 9, 9½, 9½)"/21.5 (21.5, 23, 23, 24, 24)cm

2¼ (2¾, 3, 3½, 3¾, 4¼)"/5.5 (7, 7.5, 9, 9.5, 11)cm

1½" (4cm)

7½ (7½, 8, 8, 8½, 8½)"/ 19 (19, 20, 20, 21.5, 21.5)cm

6¾ (7, 7½, 8, 8½, 9)"/17 (18, 19, 20, 21.5, 23)cm

10 (10, 10, 10½, 10½, 10½)"/ 25.5 (25.5, 25.5, 26.5, 26.5, 26.5)cm

20¼ (20½, 20½, 20½, 20½, 20½)"/51 (52, 52, 52, 52, 52)cm

27 (27½, 28, 28½, 29, 29½)"/68.5 (70, 71, 72.5, 73.5, 75)cm

30¾ (34½, 38, 41¾, 49, 52½)"/ 78 (88, 96.5, 106, 124.5, 133.5)cm

10½ (11½, 12½, 13½, 14½, 15½)"/ 26.5 (29, 31, 34, 37, 39)cm

10 (10½, 10½, 11, 11, 11½)"/25.5 (26.5, 26.5, 28, 28, 29)cm

3 (3, 3½, 3½, 4, 4)"/7.5 (7.5, 9, 9, 10, 10)cm

9¼ (9½, 10, 10½, 11, 11½)"/ 23.5 (24, 25.5, 26.5, 28, 29)cm

BACK NECK OPENING

Bind off the cutting sts, then work to end of rnd. Working back and forth, beg with a WS row.

Cont pattern as set and dec 1 st at both back neck edges every 3rd row 8 (7, 7, 6, 2, 6) times, then every 4th row 8 (8, 10, 10, 15, 12) times.

ARMHOLES

At the same time, when body measures 20¼, (20½, 20½, 20½, 20½, 20½)"/51 (52, 52, 52, 52, 52)cm from bottom edge after an odd number row of rep, shape armholes in this manner: work to 3 (3, 4, 5, 6, 6) sts before side marker, bind off the next 6 (6, 8, 10, 12, 12) sts for armhole, work next 71 (81, 87, 94, 109, 119) sts, bind off the next 6 (6, 8, 10, 12, 12) sts for armhole, then work to end of row.

Cont working front and each half of back separately.

BACK

Cont pattern and shaping back neck edge, and bind off every other row at armhole 3 sts 0 (0, 0, 0, 1, 1) times, 2 sts 0 (0, 1, 1, 2, 2) times, then 1 st 3 (5, 4, 6, 7, 8) times—12 (15, 16, 19, 20, 22) sts.

Work even until armhole measures 6³⁄₄ (7, 7¹⁄₂, 8, 8¹⁄₂, 9)"/17 (18, 19, 20.5, 21.5, 23)cm. Slip sts to holder.

Complete other side of back to match, placing neck and armhole shaping on opposite sides.

FRONT AND NECK OPENING

Cont pattern and bind off 3 sts at the beg of first 0 (0, 0, 0, 2, 2) rows, 2 sts at the beg of next 0 (0, 2, 2, 4, 4) rows, then dec 1 st at the beg and end of every other row 3 (5, 4, 6, 7, 8) times—65 (71, 75, 78, 81, 89) sts.

Work even until armhole measures 4³⁄₄ (5¹⁄₂, 6, 6¹⁄₂, 7, 7¹⁄₂)"/12 (14, 15, 16.5, 18, 19)cm.

Next row, work first 27 (30, 31, 33, 34, 37) sts, bind off the next 11 (11, 13, 12, 13, 15) sts for front neck opening, then work to end of row. Working each side of front separately, cont pattern and bind off every other row at neck edge, 3 sts 3 (3, 3, 2, 2, 3) times, then 2 sts 3 (3, 3, 4, 4, 3) times—12 (15, 16, 19, 20, 22) sts.

Work even until armhole measures 6³⁄₄ (7, 7¹⁄₂, 8, 8¹⁄₂, 9)"/17 (18, 19, 20.5, 21.5, 23)cm. Slip sts to holder. Complete other side of front to match, placing neck shaping on opposite side.

SLEEVES

With circ needle, CO 45 (47, 53, 55, 59, 61) sts. Working back and forth, knit 1 row but do not turn. Change to dpns. Join and, working in the rnd, make sure sts are not twisted. Mark beg of rnd. Purl 1 rnd, then knit 1 rnd.

Beg pattern as shown on chart, and **at the same time,** inc 1 st at the beg and end of every 16th (14th, 14th, 12th, 10th, 10th) rnd 4 (5, 5, 6, 7, 8) times, leaving 1 st between inc sts and working inc sts in garter st—53 (57, 63, 67, 73, 77) sts.

Work even until sleeve measures 10 (10¹⁄₂, 10¹⁄₂, 11, 11, 11¹⁄₂)"/25.5 (26.5, 26.5, 28, 28, 29)cm from bottom edge, ending with an odd number rnd of rep and last rnd 4 (4, 5, 6, 7, 7) sts before end of rnd.

Sleeve Cap

Bind off the next 7 (7, 9, 11, 13, 13) sts for underarm, then work to end of rnd—46 (50, 54, 56, 60, 64) sts.

Working back and forth, beg with a WS row. Cont pattern and bind off 3 sts at the beg of first 0 (4, 4, 4, 2, 2) rows,

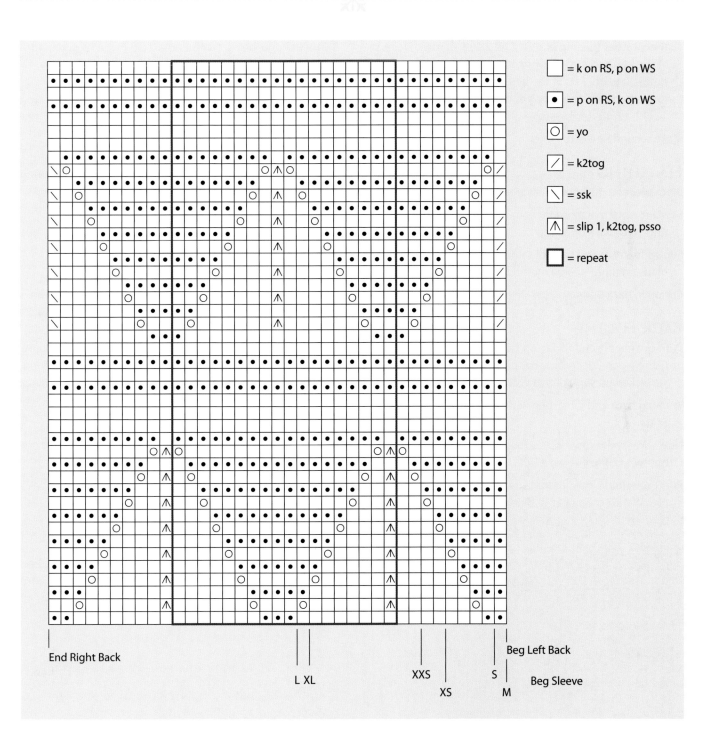

= k on RS, p on WS

• = p on RS, k on WS

O = yo

/ = k2tog

\ = ssk

Λ = slip 1, k2tog, psso

= repeat

End Right Back

L XL

XXS

XS

S

M

Beg Left Back

Beg Sleeve

then 2 sts at the beg of next 6 (2, 2, 2, 4, 4) rows. Dec 1 st at the beg and end of every other row 4 (4, 6, 6, 11, 10) times. Bind off 2 sts at the beg of next 4 (4, 4, 4, 2, 4) rows, then 3 sts at the beg of next 2 rows. Bind off rem 12 (12, 12, 14, 14, 16) sts.

Make second sleeve to match.

FINISHING

Block pieces to finished measurements.

Sew 2 rows of machine stitching along both sides of cutting sts of back opening.

Slip sts for front and back of same shoulder to dpns. Bind off using three-needle method. Rep with rem shoulder.

Cut open back opening.

BACK EDGING

With circ needle and RS facing, pick up and k11 sts per 2" (5cm) along cut edge of back opening (total number of sts picked up should be divisible by 6 + 5).

Working back and forth, beg with a WS row. Work 3 rows of St st.

Next row (eyelet row), k2, *k2tog, yo, k4; rep from * to end of row, ending last rep k3.

Purl 1 row. Purl 1 row for fold line. Purl 1 row. Work eyelet row. Work 2 rows of St st. Bind off.

Trim-cut edge, being careful not to cut machine stitching. Fold edging to inside, covering cut edge, then neatly sew to WS along edging pick-up row. Work edging along other side of back opening to match. Neatly sew lower ends of edging to bound off sts at bottom of placket opening.

Optional: Instead of binding off, cut yarn leaving a tail 3 times length of edging. Fold edging to inside, covering cut edge, then use Kitchener st to graft live sts to backs of sts that were picked up for edging. Work edging along rem back opening to match.

NECK EDGING

With circ needle and RS facing, beg at left back opening edge and pick up and k4 sts on end of back edging, 40 (40, 42, 42, 44, 44) sts along left back neck edge, 42 (42, 44, 44, 45, 45) sts along front neck, 40 (40, 42, 42, 44, 44) sts along right back edge, then 4 sts along end of edging at right back—130 (130, 136, 136, 141, 141) sts. Working back and forth, beg with a WS row and knit 2 rows. Bind off kwise on WS.

Make a twisted cord approx 40" (101.5cm) long. Beg at top of back opening, and thread cord through eyelets shoelace-fashion, and tie at bottom.

Pin sleeves into armholes, with centers of sleeves at shoulder seams, then neatly sew sleeves to body.

Zara Cardigan

This cardigan is what I like to call an I-hate-finishing sweater. Worked in the round to the beginning of the V-neck shaping, the resulting cut edges are covered by a facing knit in a finer version of the same yarn. Subtle waist shaping keeps the body from being boxy. The result is a cardigan with designer details that you can wear instead of a suit jacket. Try it in other fashion color combinations as well.

DART INC: To make 1 st slanting to left, slip left needle from front to back under horizontal strand between sts, then k tbl to twist st. To make 1 st slanting to the right, slip left needle from back to front under horizontal strand between sts, then k through the front of the loop to twist st.

DIRECTIONS

BODY

With larger circ needle and MC, CO 169 (189, 209, 229, 251, 273, 293) sts. Join and, working in the rnd, make sure sts are not twisted. Mark beg of rnd and beg rnds at center front. Place markers 2 sts out from beg and end of rnd (these 4 sts are cutting sts; purl these sts throughout and cont to include in st counts), and side markers 43 (48, 53, 58, 64, 69, 74) sts out from beg and end of rnd.

Beg St st and work until body measures 1½" (4cm) from bottom edge.

WAIST SHAPING

Work first 9 (13, 17, 21, 25, 28, 31) sts, place dart marker, k2tog, k next 56 (59, 63, 67, 72, 77, 82) sts, ssk, place dart marker, k next 31 (37, 41, 45, 49, 55, 59) sts, place dart marker, k2tog, k next 56 (59, 63, 67, 72, 77, 82) sts, ssk, place dart marker, then work rem 9 (13, 17, 21, 25, 28, 31) sts—165 (185, 205, 225, 247, 269, 289) sts. Work 5 rnds even.

Next rnd, *knit to dart marker, k2tog, knit to 2 sts before next dart marker, ssk; rep from * once more, then knit to end of rnd—161 (181, 201, 221, 243, 265, 285) sts. Rep last 6 rnds 2 (2, 2, 2, 2, 3, 3) more times—153 (173, 193, 213, 235, 253, 273) sts.

Work even until body measures approx 6½ (6½, 6½, 6½, 6½, 7, 7)"/16.5 (16.5, 16.5, 16.5, 16.5, 18, 18)cm from bottom edge. Next rnd, *work to dart marker, make 1 st

Sizes
XXS (XS, S, M, L, XL, XXL)
Sample size is Medium

Measurements
Bust: 32 (36, 40, 44, 48, 52, 54)"/81.5 (91.5, 101.5, 112, 122, 132, 137)cm
Length: 21 (21½, 22, 22½, 23, 24, 24½)"/53.5 (54.5, 56, 57, 58.5, 61, 62)cm

Yarn
Zara by Filatura di Crosa (100% extra fine merino wool superwash, 136.5 yd. [125m]/1¾ oz. [50g])
8 (9, 9, 10, 11, 12, 13) balls, color #1748 Cappuccino (MC)
Zarina by Filatura di Crosa (100% extra fine merino wool superwash, 180 yd. [160m]/1¾ oz. [50g])
1 (1, 1, 1, 1, 1, 1) ball, color #1751 Dark Rust (CC1)
1 (1, 1, 1, 1, 2, 2) ball(s), color #1775 Dark Teal (CC2)

Needles and Notions
1 each U.S. size 3 and 6 (3.25mm and 4mm) circular needles, or size needed to obtain gauge
1 set each U.S. size 3 and 6 (3.25mm and 4mm) double-pointed needles, or size needed to obtain gauge
Stitch holders
Stitch markers
Contrasting sewing thread
Matching sewing thread
14" (35.5cm) long separating zipper—Riri Bronze

Gauge
21 sts and 30 rows over St st with Zara and using larger needles = 4" (10cm)

➤ Take time to check your gauge.

Zara Cardigan

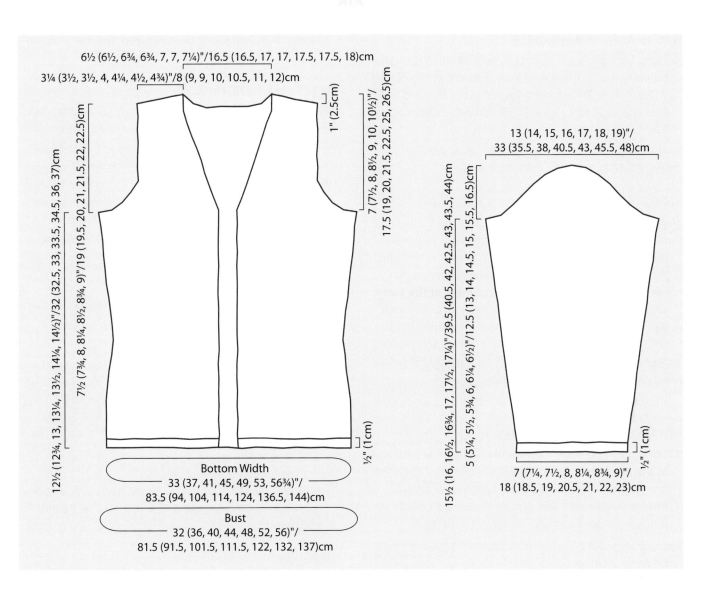

6½ (6½, 6¾, 6¾, 7, 7, 7¼)"/16.5 (16.5, 17, 17, 17.5, 17.5, 18)cm

3¼ (3½, 3½, 4, 4¼, 4½, 4¾)"/8 (9, 9, 10, 10.5, 11, 12)cm

1" (2.5cm)

7 (7½, 8, 8½, 9, 10, 10½)"/17.5 (19, 20, 21.5, 22.5, 25, 26.5)cm

12½ (13, 13¼, 13½, 14¼, 14½)"/32 (32.5, 33, 33.5, 34.5, 36, 37)cm

7½ (7¾, 8, 8¼, 8½, 8¾, 9)"/19 (19.5, 20, 21, 21.5, 22, 22.5)cm

12½ (12¾, 13, 13¼, 13½, 14¼, 14½)"/32 (32.5, 33, 33.5, 34.5, 36, 37)cm

½" (1cm)

Bottom Width
33 (37, 41, 45, 49, 53, 56¾)"/
83.5 (94, 104, 114, 124, 136.5, 144)cm

Bust
32 (36, 40, 44, 48, 52, 56)"/
81.5 (91.5, 101.5, 111.5, 122, 132, 137)cm

13 (14, 15, 16, 17, 18, 19)"/
33 (35.5, 38, 40.5, 43, 45.5, 48)cm

15½ (16, 16½, 16¾, 17, 17½, 17¼)"/39.5 (40.5, 42, 42.5, 43, 43.5, 44)cm

5 (5¼, 5½, 5¾, 6, 6¼, 6½)"/12.5 (13, 14, 14.5, 15, 15.5, 16.5)cm

½" (1cm)

7 (7¼, 7½, 8, 8¼, 8¾, 9)"/
18 (18.5, 19, 20.5, 21, 22, 23)cm

slanting to the left, work to next dart marker, make 1 st slanting to the right; rep from * once more, then work to end of row—157 (177, 197, 217, 239, 257, 277) sts. Knit 15 rnds even. Rep last 16 rnds 1 (1, 1, 1, 1, 2, 2) more time(s), then work 1 more inc rnd—165 (185, 205, 225, 247, 269, 289) sts.

Work even until body measures 12 (12¼, 12½, 12¾, 13, 13¾, 14)"/30.5 (31, 32, 32.5, 33, 35, 35.5)cm from bottom edge.

Armholes

Next rnd: Work to 3 (3, 4, 4, 5, 5, 6) sts before side marker, bind off the next 6 (6, 8, 8, 10, 10, 12) sts for armhole, knit to 3 (3, 4, 4, 5, 5, 6) sts before next side marker, bind off the next 6 (6, 8, 8, 10, 10, 12) sts for armhole, then work to end of rnd—77 (87, 95, 105, 113, 125, 133) sts rem for back, and 76 (86, 94, 104, 114, 124, 132) sts rem for front, including cutting sts. Cont working front and back of body separately.

BACK AND ARMHOLES

Working back and forth, cont St st and bind off 3 sts at the beg of first 0 (2, 2, 2, 2, 4, 4) rows, 2 sts at the beg of next 2 (2, 4, 4, 4, 4, 6) rows, then dec 1 st at the beg and end of every other row 2 (3, 4, 7, 7, 9, 9) times—69 (71, 73, 77, 85, 87, 91) sts.

Work even until armhole measures $6^1/_2$ ($6^3/_4$, 7, $7^1/_4$, $7^1/_2$, $7^3/_4$, 8)"/16.5 (17, 18, 18.5, 19, 19.5, 20.5)cm.

NECK OPENING AND SHOULDERS

Work first 24 (25, 25, 27, 30, 31, 32) sts, bind off the next 21 (21, 23, 23, 25, 25, 27) sts for neck opening, then work next 17 (18, 18, 19, 20, 22, 23) sts. Wrap next st and turn. Work back to neck edge. Bind off every other row at neck edge, 3 sts once, then 2 sts once, and **at the same time,** work 6 (7, 7, 7, 8, 9, 9) fewer sts at shoulder once, wrapping next st and turning. Work 1 row over rem 19 (20, 20, 22, 25, 26, 27) sts, picking up wraps and working them tog with the sts they wrapped. Slip sts to st holder.

Complete other side of back to match, placing neck and shoulder shaping on opposite sides.

FRONT AND NECK OPENING

Working back and forth, shape armholes same as back and, **at the same time,** when front measures $13^1/_2$" (34.5cm) from bottom edge, bind off the 4 cuttings at center front and work each side of front separately. Cont St st, armhole shaping and dec 1 st at neck as follows:

Size XXS: alternating 3rd row 6 times, then 4th row 6 times, then every 4th row once more—19 sts.

Sizes XS, S, M, L: every 4th row 13 (14, 14, 16) times—20 (20, 22, 25) sts.

Sizes XL, XXL: alternating 4th row 5 (6) times, then 5th row 5 (6) times, then every 4th row 5 (4) times—26 (27) sts.

All sizes: Work even until armhole measures $6^1/_2$ ($6^3/_4$, 7, $7^1/_4$, $7^1/_2$, $7^3/_4$, 8)"/16.5 (17, 18, 18.5, 19, 19.5, 20.5)cm, ending last row at neck edge. Shape shoulder same as back, then slip sts to st holders. Complete other side of front to match, placing armhole, neck, and shoulder shaping on opposite sides.

BOTTOM EDGING

With smaller circ needle, CC1 and with RS facing. Beg with 3rd st from center front and pick up and k23 sts per 4" (10cm) along CO edge to 3rd st before center front (the 4 cutting sts should be between picked up sts).

Working back and forth, beg with a WS row and knit 1 row. Change to CC2 and work 3 rows of St st. Knit 1 row on WS for fold line. Work 3 rows of St st, then bind off neatly. Fold edging to inside along fold line and sew neatly to WS.

SLEEVES

With larger dpns and MC, CO 36 (38, 40, 42, 44, 46, 48) sts. Join and, working in the rnd, make sure sts are not twisted. Mark beg of rnd.

Beg St st and, **at the same time,** inc 1 st at the beg and end of every 7th rnd 10 (0, 0, 0, 0, 0, 0) times, every 6th rnd 6 (18, 15, 10, 10, 0, 0) times, every 5th rnd 0 (0, 5, 11, 12, 24, 18) times, then every 4th rnd 0 (0, 0, 0, 0, 0, 8) times, leaving 2 sts between inc sts—68 (74, 80, 84, 88, 94, 100) sts.

Work even until sleeve measures 15 ($15^1/_2$, 16, $16^1/_4$, $16^1/_2$, 17, $16^3/_4$)"/38 (39.5, 40.5, 41.5, 42, 43, 42.5)cm from bottom edge, ending last rnd 3 (3, 4, 4, 5, 5, 6) sts before end of rnd.

Sleeve Cap

Bind off the next 6 (6, 8, 8, 10, 10, 12) sts for underarm, then knit to end of rnd—62 (68, 72, 76, 78, 84, 88) sts.

Working back and forth, cont St st and bind off 3 sts at the beg of first 4 rows, 2 sts at the beg of next 4 (4, 6, 6, 6, 6, 6) rows. Dec 1 st at the beg and end of every other row 11 (11, 11, 12, 13, 13, 13) times. Bind off 2 sts at the beg of next 2 (2, 2, 2, 2, 4, 6) rows, 3 sts at the beg of next 0 (2, 2, 2, 2, 2, 2) rows, then 4 sts at the beg of next 2 rows. Bind off rem 8 (8, 8, 10, 10, 12, 12) sts.

Sleeve Edging

With smaller dpns, CC1 and with RS facing, pick up and k40 (41, 43, 45, 47, 50, 52) sts along CO edge. Join and, working in the rnd, mark beg of rnd. Purl 1 rnd. Change to CC2 and knit 3 rnds. Purl 1 rnd for fold line. Knit 3 rnds, then bind off loosely. Fold edging to inside along fold line and sew neatly to WS.

Make second sleeve to match.

FINISHING

Sew 2 rows of machine stitching along each side of front cutting sts. Cut open front opening.

Slip sts from front and back of one shoulder to larger needles. Bind off using three-needle method. If necessary to close gaps between sts where short rows were worked, lift strand of yarn between sts and slip it, twisted, onto left needle, and work tog with next st. Block pieces to finished measurements; steam blocking works best with this yarn.

FRONT EDGING

With smaller circ needle, CC1 and with RS facing, beg at lower edge of right front and pick up and knit 23 sts per 4" (10cm) along front and back neck edges to lower edge of left front. Place markers on both sides of where front V-neck shaping starts.

Working back and forth, beg with a WS row and knit 1 row. Change to CC2 and work 3 rows of St st. Knit 1 row on WS for fold line. Work 4 rows of St st and bind off 3 sts at beg of last row.

Next row (RS): Bind off 3 sts, knit to first marker, bind off sts between markers, then knit to end of row.

Working each side of front separately, work 2 rows of St st. Change to CC1. Work 4 rows of reverse St st. Bind off neatly.

ZIPPER

Turn cut edge of front toward front edging. Fold edging to inside along fold line along entire front and neck edge. Neatly sew bound-off edge to WS along shaped edges of front and back neck, leaving open where zipper is to be inserted.

Pin zipper into one side of front opening, with center of zipper teeth at fold edge. Using matching sewing thread, neatly sew zipper to front opening, using back st through front and zipper tape. Sew other side of zipper into opening in same manner. (**Hint:** To make sure front edges meet at center of zipper, baste fold edges of front edging tog using a simple running st through purl ridges on both sides.)

On inside, fold facing back over zipper tape, making sure zipper will not catch bound-off edge, and use 1st row of rev St st as fold line. Neatly sew bound-off edge to back of zipper tape.

Pin fold edge to WS and neatly sew down.

Pin sleeves into armholes, then neatly sew to body.

Sizes
XS (S, M, L, XL)
Sample size is Small.

Measurements
Bust: 35 (39, 43, 47, 51)"/89 (99, 109, 119.5, 129.5)cm

Length: 27 (27$^1/_2$, 28, 28$^1/_2$, 29)"/68.5 (70, 71, 72.5, 73.5)cm

Yarns
Bouclé Mohair by Be Sweet Products (100% mohair, 120 yd. [110m]/1$^3/_4$ oz. [50g])

7 (8, 8, 9, 10) skeins, color Deep Turquoise (MC)

Extra Fine Mohair by Be Sweet Products (100% mohair, 230 yd. [211m]/$^7/_8$ oz. [25g])

1 (1, 1, 1, 1) skein, color Green Potion (CC)

Needles and Notions
1 U.S. size 9 (5.5mm) circular needles, or size needed to obtain gauge

1 U.S. size 6 (4mm) circular needle

1 set each U.S. sizes 6 and 9 (4mm and 5.5mm) double-pointed needles

Stitch holders

Stitch markers

Contrasting sewing thread

3 buttons, $^3/_4$" (19mm)—Muench Yarns #1514 Rainbow Swiss Rectangle

Gauge
15 sts and 24 rnds over St st using larger needles = 4" (10cm)

▶ Take time to check your gauge.

Bouclé Mohair Cardigan

Although plain in terms of stitch patterns (just garter and stockinette), this amazing cardigan has loads of potential for customizing—shorten it, change colors, choose colors that are very similar, use different buttons. It's an easy-to-knit piece with class. The narrow facings worked along the cut edges are done in a finer yarn, so keep those edges from becoming extremely bulky. A single layer collar slouches just a little for a little softness at the neck, and can easily be shortened.

DIRECTIONS

BODY
With larger circular needle and MC, CO 128 (140, 156, 172, 188) sts. Working back and forth, knit 6 rows and CO 4 new sts at end of last row—132 (144, 160, 176, 192) sts; these are cutting sts, work in St st throughout and cont to include in st counts.

Join and, working in the rnd, make sure sts are not twisted. Mark beg of rnd and beg rnds at center of cutting sts. Place side markers 34 (37, 41, 45, 49) sts out from beg and end of rnd. Beg St st and work until body measures 18$^3/_4$ (19, 19$^1/_4$, 19$^1/_2$, 19$^3/_4$)"/47.5 (48.5, 49, 49.5, 50)cm from bottom edge.

ARMHOLES
Next rnd, k32 (34, 37, 40, 43) sts, bind off next 4 (6, 8, 10, 12) sts for armhole, knit next 60 (64, 70, 76, 82) sts, bind off next 4 (6, 8, 10, 12) sts for armhole, then knit to end of rnd—64 (68, 74, 80, 86) sts rem for front and 60 (64, 70, 76, 82) sts rem for back. Cont working front and back of body separately.

FRONT
With RS facing, cut yarn and slip 32 (34, 37, 40, 43) sts of left front from right needle to left needle. Reattach yarn and, working back and forth, beg rows at armholes. Cont St st and dec 1 st at the beg and end of every other row 4 (4, 5, 6, 7) times—56 (60, 64, 68, 72) sts, including cutting sts.

Work even until armhole measures approx 3$^3/_4$ (4, 4$^1/_4$, 4$^1/_4$, 4$^1/_2$)"/9.5 (10, 11, 11, 11.5) cm, ending with a WS row.

Next row, k32 (34, 36, 38, 40) sts, k2tog, yo for buttonhole, then knit to end of row. Work until armhole measures approx 8 (8$^1/_4$, 8$^1/_2$, 8$^3/_4$, 9)"/20.5 (21, 21.5, 22, 23)cm.

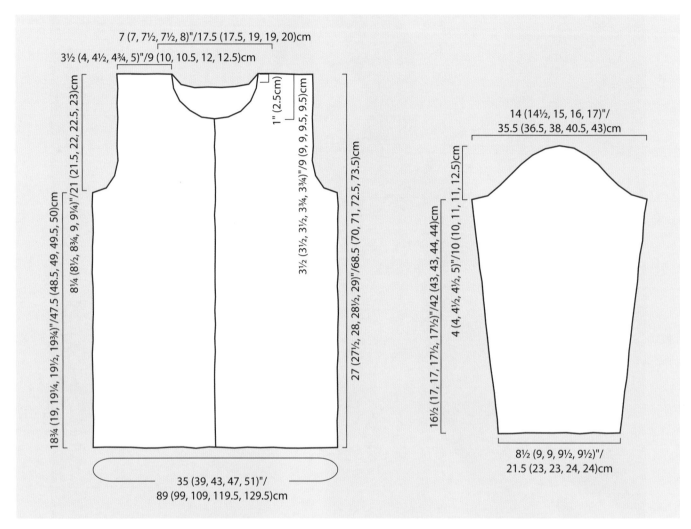

Next row, work 13 (15, 16, 18, 19) sts, bind off the next 30 (30, 32, 32, 34) sts for neck opening, then work to end of row. Slip rem 13 (15, 16, 18, 19) sts on each shoulder to separate st holders.

BACK

Working back and forth, cont St st and dec 1 st at the beg and end of every other row 4 (4, 5, 6, 7) times—52 (56, 60, 64, 68) sts. Work even until armhole measures approx 8 (8¼, 8½, 8¾, 9)"/20.5 (21, 21.5, 22, 23)cm.

Next row, work 13 (15, 16, 18, 19) sts, bind off the next 26 (26, 28, 28, 30) sts for neck opening, then work to end of row. Slip rem 13 (15, 16, 18, 19) sts on each shoulder on separate st holders.

SLEEVES

With dpns and MC, CO 32 (34, 34, 36, 36) sts. Join and, working in the rnd, make sure sts are not twisted. Mark beg of rnd and work 6 rnds of garter st (*knit 1 rnd, purl 1 rnd; rep from *).

Beg St st and, **at the same time,** inc 1 st at the beg and end rnd every 1½" (4cm) 10 (10, 7, 5, 0) times, every 1¼" (3cm) 0 (0, 4, 7, 7) times, then every 1" (2.5cm) 0 (0, 0, 0, 7) times, leaving 2 sts between inc sts—52 (54, 56, 60, 64) sts.

Work even until sleeve measures 16½ (17, 17, 17½, 17½)"/42 (43, 43, 44.5, 44.5)cm from bottom edge, ending last rnd 2 (3, 4, 5, 6) sts before end of rnd.

Sleeve Cap

Bind off the next 4 (6, 8, 10, 12) sts for underarm, then knit to end of rnd—48 (48, 48, 50, 52) sts.

Working back and forth, cont St st and bind off 3 sts at the beg of first 2 rows, then 2 sts at the beg of next 4 (4, 2, 2, 2) rows.

Dec 1 st at the beg and end of every other row 6 (7, 9, 8, 10) times.

Bind off 2 sts at the beg of next 4 (2, 2, 4, 2) rows, then 3 sts at the beg of next 2 rows. Bind off rem 8 (10, 10, 10, 12) sts.

Make second sleeve to match.

FINISHING

Block pieces to finished measurements.

Mark front for center opening and front neck; neck should be 3½ (3½, 3½, 3¾, 3¾)"/9 (9, 9, 9.5, 9.5)cm deep, and width is between sts on holders. Mark back for back neck edge; neck should be approx 1" (2.5cm) deep, and width is between sts on holders.

Sew 2 rows of machine stitching on both sides of front opening, and along front and back neck lines, making sure to sew above marked neck lines. Cut open along center front opening only.

Slip sts for front and back of one shoulder to dpns and work three-needle bind-off. Rep with rem shoulder.

NECK BINDING

With smaller circ needle, 2 strands of CC held tog, and with RS facing, beg at right front edge and pick up and k21 sts per 4" (10cm) along neck edge, picking up sts below machine stitching. Working back and forth, work 2 rows of St st. Knit1 row on WS for fold line. Work 2 rows of St st. Bind off loosely.

Carefully trim excess out of neck opening, making sure to not cut machine stitching. Fold neck binding over cut edge, then sew to WS along pick-up row.

COLLAR

With larger circ needle, 1 strand of MC and with RS facing, pick up and k15 sts per 4" (10cm) along fold edge of neck binding. Working back and forth, beg with a WS row and work 4½ (5, 5, 5, 5)"/11.5 (12.5, 12.5, 12.5, 12.5)cm of St st. **At the same time,** work rem buttonholes, 2 sts in from right front edge when collar measures approx 1" (2.5cm), then when collar measures approx 3 (3½, 3½, 3½, 3½)"/7.5 (9, 9, 9, 9)cm. When collar measures finished length, Bind off loosely.

COLLAR EDGING

With smaller circ needle, 2 strands of CC held tog, and with RS facing, beg at right front edge and pick up and k21 sts per 4" (10cm) along top edge of collar. Working back and forth, work 5 rows of St st. Bind off loosely. Fold edging to inside along middle of edging, then sew neatly to WS along pick-up row.

FRONT EDGING

With smaller circ needle, 2 strands of CC held tog, and with RS facing, beg at bottom of right front edge and pick up and k21 sts per 4" (10cm) along front opening edge, end of collar, and collar edging. Working back and forth, work 5 rows of St st. Bind off loosely. Trim cut edge, making sure to not cut machine stitching. Fold edging to inside along middle of edging and covering cut edge of front. Sew neatly to WS along pick-up row, and sew ends of edging closed. Work edging along left front and end of collar in same manner.

Pin sleeves into armholes, then sew to body. Sew buttons to left front under buttonholes.

Ambrosia Vest

Sizes
XS (S, M, L, XL, XXL)
Sample size is Small

Measurements
Bust: 31 (35, 39, 43, 47, 52)"/79 (89, 99, 109, 119.5, 132)cm
Length: 19 (19¹⁄₂, 19³⁄₄, 20, 20¹⁄₄, 20¹⁄₂)"/48.5 (49.5, 50, 51, 51.5, 52)cm

Yarn
Ambrosia by Knit One, Crochet Too (70% alpaca/20% silk/10% cashmere, 137 yd. [125m]/1³⁄₄ oz. [50g])
4 (5, 6, 6, 7, 8) balls, color #249 Garnet (MC)
3 (3, 3, 3, 4, 4) balls, color #887 Chocolate (CC1)
1 (1, 1, 1, 1, 1) ball, color #591 Spruce (CC2)

Needles and Notions
1 each U.S. size 2 and 3 (2.75mm and 3.25mm) circular needles, or size needed to obtain gauge
Stitch holders
Stitch markers
Contrasting sewing thread
4 buttons, ¹⁄₂" (12.7mm)—Danforth Pewter #10-1089 Lucky

Gauge
26 sts and 34 rows over St st using larger needles = 4" (10cm)
27 sts and 36 rows over color work pattern using smaller needles = 4" (10cm)
➤ Take time to check your gauge.

Aving to try, or experiment with a color pattern that's inspired creativity. Working in the round on smaller needles always seems to go more quickly than working back and forth, even over a large number of stitches. The patterned portion of the neck and front edging is knit in the round to make knitting the color-stranded pattern easier to work, and the scallops of the picot edges add a decidedly feminine touch to the edgings.

NOTE The front of the vest is worked straight without shaping along the front edge. The shaping of front edges is achieved by picking up fewer stitches per inch/centimeter along the front edge than around the upper edge of the front opening and back neck.

FULL-FASHION DEC: Knit 2 stitches together before each dart marker, and ssk after each dart marker. Work full-fashion shaping at armholes in same manner, working decreases before and after cutting stitches.

MAKE 1 INC (m1): Lift horizontal strand between last stitch just worked and next stitch on left needle, then knit through the back of the loop.

DIRECTIONS
BODY
With smaller needle and CC1, CO 175 (197, 223, 249, 275, 305) sts. Working back and forth, beg with a WS row and work 17 rows of St st, inc 8 sts evenly spaced across last row—183 (205, 231, 257, 283, 313) sts.

Next row (RS), work fold line in this manner: K1, *yo, k2tog; rep from * to end of row, and CO 4 new sts at end of row (these are cutting sts; work in CC1 throughout for Border Pattern and exclude from st counts).

Join and, working in the rnd, make sure sts are not twisted. Mark beg of rnd and beg rnds at center of cutting sts. Work Border Pattern, beg each size as shown on chart (page 107), and work 16-st rep to cutting sts at end of rnd.

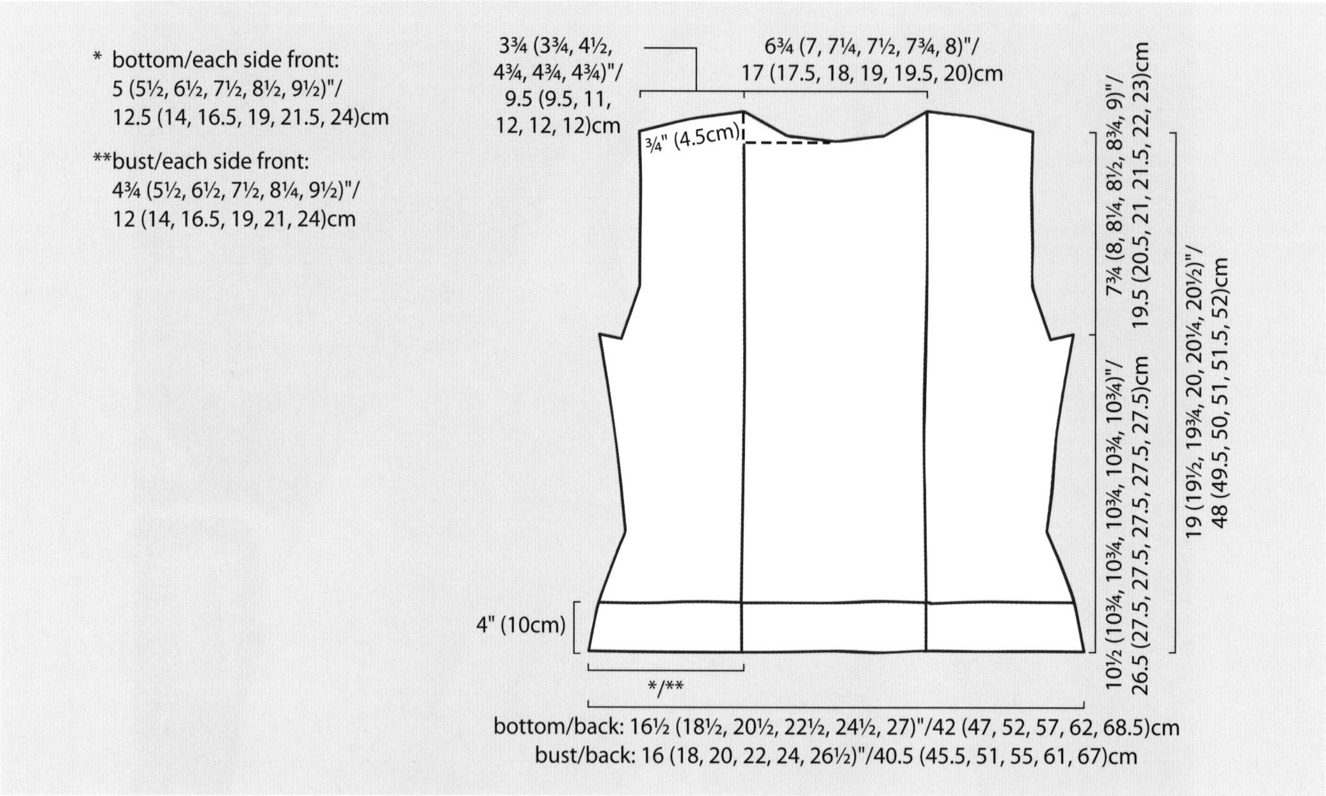
* bottom/each side front:
5 (5½, 6½, 7½, 8½, 9½)"/
12.5 (14, 16.5, 19, 21.5, 24)cm
**bust/each side front:
4¾ (5½, 6½, 7½, 8¼, 9½)"/
12 (14, 16.5, 19, 21, 24)cm
3¾ (3¾, 4½, 4¾, 4¾, 4¾)"/ 9.5 (9.5, 11, 12, 12, 12)cm
6¾ (7, 7¼, 7½, 7¾, 8)"/ 17 (17.5, 18, 19, 19.5, 20)cm
¾" (4.5cm)
7¾ (8, 8¼, 8½, 8¾, 9)"/ 19.5 (20.5, 21, 21.5, 22, 23)cm
19 (19½, 19¾, 20, 20¼, 20½)"/ 48 (49.5, 50, 51, 51.5, 52)cm
10½ (10¾, 10¾, 10¾, 10¾, 10¾)"/ 26.5 (27.5, 27.5, 27.5, 27.5, 27.5)cm
4" (10cm)
*/**
bottom/back: 16½ (18½, 20½, 22½, 24½, 27)"/42 (47, 52, 57, 62, 68.5)cm
bust/back: 16 (18, 20, 22, 24, 26½)"/40.5 (45.5, 51, 55, 61, 67)cm

Change to larger needle and MC. Knit 1 rnd and dec 8 sts evenly spaced across rnd—175 (197, 223, 249, 275, 305) sts.

Place front dart markers 7 sts out from both sides of cutting sts, and back dart markers 61 (71, 84, 95, 108, 122) sts out from both sides of cutting sts (53 [55, 55, 59, 59, 61] sts between markers on back).

DARTS

Knit 3 rnds. Next rnd, knit to first dart marker, k2tog, (knit to 2 sts before next dart marker, ssk, k1, k2tog) twice, knit to last dart marker, ssk, then knit to end of rnd—169 (191, 217, 243, 269, 299) sts. Rep these 4 rows 3 more times—151 (173, 199, 225, 251, 281) sts.

Knit 10 rnds even.

Next rnd, work to first dart marker, m1, (knit to next dart marker, m1, k1, m1 st) twice, knit to last dart marker, m1 st, then knit to end of rnd—157 (179, 205, 231, 257, 287) sts. Knit 12 rnds even. Rep last 13 rnds once more, then work 1 more inc rnd—169 (191, 217, 243, 269, 299) sts.

Work even until body measures 10½ (10¾, 10¾, 10¾, 10¾, 10¾)"/26.5 (27.5, 27.5, 27.5, 27.5, 27.5)cm from fold line.

ARMHOLES

Next rnd, knit the cutting sts and first 27 (31, 37, 42, 44, 46) sts, bind off the next 9 (10, 10, 12, 20, 30) sts for armhole, knit next 97 (109, 123, 135, 141, 147) sts, bind off the next 9 (10, 10, 12, 20, 30) sts for armhole, then knit to end of rnd—151 (171, 197, 219, 229, 239) sts.

Next rnd, CO 4 cutting sts over bind-off sts of previous rnd.

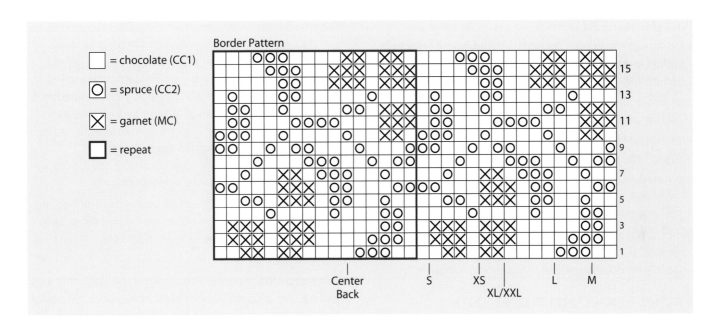

Border Pattern

☐ = chocolate (CC1)

Ⓞ = spruce (CC2)

☒ = garnet (MC)

☐ = repeat

Center
Back

S   XS   L   M
XL/XXL

Cont St st and, **at the same time**, dec 1 st, 1 st in from cutting sts before and after each armhole every other rnd 2 (3, 3, 5, 7, 8) times, then every 4th rnd 0 (3, 5, 6, 6, 7) times, working full fashion dec in same manner as for darts—143 (147, 165, 175, 177, 179) sts; 25 (25, 29, 31, 31, 31) sts for each front and 93 (97, 107, 113, 115, 117) sts for back.

Work even until armhole measures 7^{3}/$_{4}$ (8, 8^{1}/$_{4}$, 8^{1}/$_{2}$, 8^{3}/$_{4}$, 9)"/19.5 (20.5, 21, 21.5, 22, 23)cm, ending last rnd before center front cutting sts.

SHOULDER SHAPING

Bind off the cutting sts at center front and at each armhole.

Left shoulder: Work 18 (18, 21, 23, 23, 23) sts, then wrap next st and turn. Slip first st and tighten it slightly, then work back to neck edge. Next row, work 12 (12, 14, 15, 15, 15) sts, then wrap next st and turn. Slip first st and tighten it slightly, then work back to neck edge. Next row, work 6 (6, 7, 7, 7, 7) sts, then wrap next st and turn. Slip first st and tighten it slightly, then work back to neck edge. Work 1 row over all sts, picking up wraps and working them tog with the sts they wrapped.

Slip sts to holder and work right front to match.

BACK

Work 32 (33, 37, 39, 39, 39) sts, bind off the next 29 (31, 33, 35, 37, 39) sts for neck opening, work 25 (26, 29, 31, 31, 31) sts, then wrap and turn. Working each side of back separately, shape shoulders same as front and, **at the same time,** bind off at back neck edges, 3 (4, 4, 4, 4, 4) sts once, then 2 sts twice. Work 1 row over rem sts, picking up wraps and working them tog with the sts they wrapped. Slip rem 25 (25, 29, 31, 31, 31) sts to st holder.

FINISHING

Sew 2 rows of machine stitching along both sides of cutting sts for front and armhole openings.

Cut open armholes and front opening.

Slip sts for front and back of one shoulder to larger needles, with neck edges at ends of needle. Cast off using two-needle method with live sts.

Block to finished measurements. Fold lower edge to inside along fold line and sew neatly to WS.

ARMHOLE EDGINGS

With smaller circ needle, MC and RS facing, beg at bottom of armhole and pick up and k14 sts per 2" (5cm) along armhole edge, making sure to pick up an even number of sts.

Join and, working in the rnd, mark beg of rnd and beg rnds at bottom of armhole.

Knit 2 rnds. Work a picot rnd for fold line (*yo, k2tog; rep from * to end). Knit 3 rnds.

Place markers at corners of underarm (sts bound off at beg of armhole). Knit 5 more rnds and, **at the same time,** inc 1 st at each marker every other rnd 3 times. Bind off loosely.

Turn cut edges of armholes toward body. Fold facing toward body, covering cut edges, then neatly sew facing to WS. Work edging along rem armhole to match.

FRONT EDGE AND NECKBAND

Place markers 3¹⁄₂" (9cm) from shoulders on each side of front.

With smaller needle, MC and RS facing, CO 3 sts, pick up and k7 sts per 1" (2.5cm) along end of band at lower right edge, working through both layers, pick up and k12 sts per 2" (5cm) along right front edge to marker, pick up and k14 sts per 2" (5cm) along top of right front edge, back neck and top of left front edge to marker, pick up and k12 sts per 2" (5cm) from marker to top of band at lower-left edge, pick up and k7 sts per 1" (2.5cm) along lower-left edge, then CO 3 sts. Total number of sts picked up should be divisible by 8.

Join and, working in the rnd, mark beg of rnd and beg rnds at center of CO sts (the 6 CO sts are cutting sts; work in CC1 throughout and exclude from pattern).

Change to CC1 and knit 1 rnd.

Work first 3 rnds of Border Pattern. Next rnd, work first 3 sts of pattern, bind off 2 sts for buttonhole, work 9 sts, bind off 2 sts for buttonhole, then work to end. Next rnd, CO 2 new sts over bound-off sts of previous rnd. Work 7 more rnds of pattern. Next rnd, make buttonholes same as for 4th rnd. Complete pattern.

Knit 1 rnd with CC1 and bind off cutting sts.

Beg working back and forth and beg with a RS row. Work a picot row for fold line. Work 17 rows of St st, working another set of buttonholes to match front of band. Bind off loosely.

Sew 2 rows of machine stitching along both sides of cutting sts at bottom of opening. Cut between stitching.

Turn lower ends of front band to inside so that machine stitching will be covered by facing. Baste to WS. Fold facing to inside along fold line, lining up buttonholes. Neatly sew facing to WS and lower edges closed.

Sew around buttonholes, working through both front and facing to attach layers, and reinforce the buttonholes, making sure that buttons can slip through the openings. Try on the vest and mark position of buttons; place the buttons at an angle in order to allow the lower edge to curve the way it will want to do. Sew buttons to left front band as marked.

Block front edge and neckband.

Green Line Cabled Pullover

Cabled sweaters are always fun to knit, especially as you watch the lines of the cables snake their way up the piece. This design features sleeves that are worked from the shoulder down, beginning with short rows to shape the sleeve cap. Facings are added to both the armholes and front neck edges that keep bulk along the cut edges to a minimum.

The soft yarn used here will make this a warm and comfy sweater to throw on during those chilly autumn days.

DIRECTIONS

BODY

With smaller circ needle, CO 200 (216, 232, 252, 272, 292) sts. Join and, working in the rnd, make sure sts are not twisted. Mark beg of rnd. Work 5" (12.5cm) of k2, p2 rib.

Next rnd, cont rib and inc in this manner: *work 23 (27, 31, 36, 41, 46) sts, m1, work 4 sts, m1, work 20 sts, m1, work 6 sts, m1, work 20 sts, m1, work 4 sts, m1, work 23 (27, 31, 36, 41, 46) sts; rep from * once more—212 (228, 244, 264, 284, 304) sts.

Change to larger circ needle and place side markers at the beg of rnd and after 106 (114, 122, 132, 142, 152) sts.

Set pattern across next rnd in this manner: p13 (17, 21, 26, 31, 36), work Cable Pattern over next 80 sts, p26 (34, 42, 52, 62, 72), work Cable Pattern over next 80 sts, then p rem 13 (17, 21, 26, 31, 36) sts.

Cont working as est until body measures 14¼ (14½, 15, 15¼, 15¾, 16)"/36 (37, 38, 38.5, 40, 40.5)cm from bottom of rib.

FRONT NECK OPENING

Next rnd, work first 41 (45, 49, 54, 59, 64) sts, bind off the next 24 sts for front neck opening, then work to end of rnd—188 (204, 220, 240, 260, 280) sts. CO 4 new sts over bound-off sts of previous rnd (these are cutting sts; work in St st throughout and exclude from st counts).

Cont pattern and dec 1 st on each side of neck edge, cutting sts every 4th rnd 10 (11, 11, 12, 12, 13) times.

Sizes
XS (S, M, L, XL, XXL)
Sample size is Small

Measurements
Bust: 35½ (39, 42¾, 46¼, 51½, 56)"/90 (99, 108.5, 117.5, 131, 142)cm
Body Length: 23 (23½, 24, 24½, 25, 25½)"/58.5 (59.5, 61, 62, 63.5, 65)cm
Sleeve Length to Underarm: 17½ (18, 18, 18¼, 18½, 18¼)"/44.5 (45.5, 45.5, 46.5, 47, 46.5)cm

Yarn
Green Line DK by Lorna's Laces (100% organic merino wool, 145 yd. [133m]/2 oz. [56.7g])
8 (9, 10, 10, 11, 12) skeins, color 38ns Brick

Needles and Notions
1 each U.S. size 7 and 8 (4.5mm and 5mm) circular needles, or size needed to obtain gauge
1 set each U.S. size 7 and 8 (4.5mm and 5mm) double-pointed needles, or size needed to obtain gauge
Cable needle
Stitch markers
Contrasting sewing thread

Gauge
18 sts and 26 rows over St st using larger needles = 4" (10cm); each cable should measure approx 4" (10cm) wide at widest point.

➤ Take time to check your gauge.

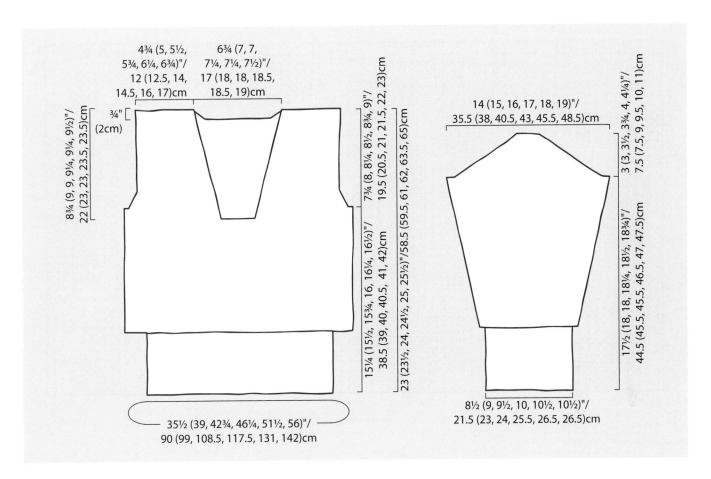

At the same time, when body measures 15¼ (15½, 15¾, 16, 16¼, 16½)"/38.5 (39.5, 40, 40.5, 41.5, 42)cm from bottom of rib, end last rnd 2 (2, 4, 5, 6, 6) sts before end of rnd and shape armholes.

ARMHOLES

Bind off the next 4 (4, 8, 10, 12, 12) sts for armhole, work to 2 (2, 4, 5, 6, 6) sts before next side marker, bind off the next 4 (4, 8, 10, 12, 12) sts for armhole, then work to end of rnd. CO 4 cutting sts over each armhole, and cont working in the rnd. **At the same time,** dec 1 st, 1 st in from armhole cutting sts, every 3rd rnd 0 (2, 0, 2, 2, 0) times, then every other rnd 0 (2, 0, 0, 0, 8) times—98 (102, 106, 110, 116, 120) sts rem on back.

When front neck shaping is complete, 142 (158, 166, 172, 184, 190) sts rem—27 (28, 30, 31, 34, 35) sts on each side of front, and 98 (102, 106, 110, 116, 120) sts on back. Work even until body measures approx 22¼ (22¾, 23¼, 23¾, 24¼, 24¾)"/56.5 (58, 59, 60.5, 61.5, 63)cm from bottom of rib, ending last rnd with non-cabling rnd (any rem cable rows will need to be worked on the RS).

BACK NECK OPENING

Work front sts and bind off front cutting sts, then work first 29 (30, 32, 33, 36, 37) sts of back as est, bind off the next 40 (42, 42, 44, 44, 46) sts for back neck opening, then work to end of rnd. Working each side of body separately, over both front and back, work 4 more rows and

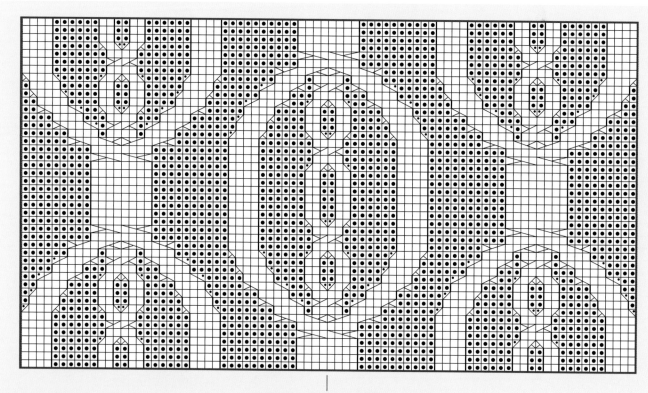

Center of Front and Back

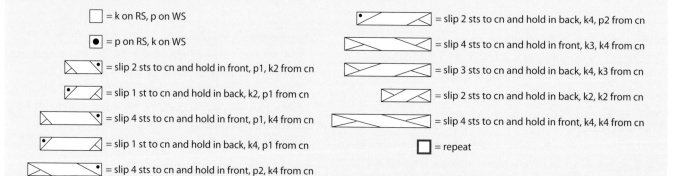

bind off at back neck edge, 2 sts once, and bind off the 4 armhole cutting sts on last row—27 (28, 30, 31, 34, 35) sts rem for each shoulder. Work 1 row of reverse St st over all sts, then bind off. Complete other side of body to match.

Sew 2 rows of machine stitching along each side of cutting sts at armholes and front neck opening. Cut open armholes. Sew shoulders tog on RS using whip st through purl row at top of shoulders.

SLEEVES

NOTE

The sleeves are worked in reverse St st. If desired, turn sleeve with WS facing and knit every rnd; make sure to add new skeins on knit side of work.

With larger circ needle or dpns and RS facing, beg at bottom of armhole and pick up and k66 (70, 74, 78, 82, 86) sts along armhole edge, then turn. Working back and forth, beg with a WS row and k38 (40, 42, 44, 46, 48) sts, wrap next st, then turn. Slip first st and tighten it slightly, p9 sts, wrap next st, then turn. Slip first st and tighten it slightly, k12 (12, 12, 12, 12, 11) sts, wrap next st, then turn. Slip first st and tighten it slightly, p15 (15, 15, 15, 15, 13) sts, wrap next st, then turn. Slip first st and tighten it slightly, k18 (18, 18, 18, 18, 15) sts, wrap next st, then turn. Slip first st and tighten it slightly, p21 (21, 21, 21, 21, 17) sts, wrap next st, then turn.

Cont working in this manner, working an extra 3 sts at end of every row 6 (6, 4, 1, 0, 0) times for each side, then an extra 2 sts at end of every row 0 (0, 3, 7, 9, 10) times for each side—8 (12, 16, 22, 26, 32) sts rem unworked at bottom of armhole.

Work to end of next 2 rows, then join and beg working in the rnd. Mark beg of rnd.

Cont working reverse St st, and, **at the same time,** dec 1 st at the beg and end of 1st rnd, then every 7th rnd 0 (6, 0, 0, 0, 0) times, every 6th rnd 13 (6, 13, 10, 8, 0) times, then every 5th rnd 0 (0, 0, 4, 7, 17) times, leaving 2 sts

between dec sts—38 (44, 46, 48, 50, 50) sts. Change to dpns when too few sts rem to work on circ needle.

Work even until sleeve measures 12½ (13, 13, 13¼, 13½, 13¼)"/32 (33, 33, 33.5, 34.5, 33.5)cm from bottom of armhole and dec 2 (4, 2, 4, 2, 2) sts evenly spaced across last rnd—36 (40, 44, 44, 48, 48) sts.

Change to smaller dpns. Beg k2, p2 rib and work until cuff measures 5" (12.5cm). Bind off loosely in rib.

Make second sleeve to match.

Sleeve Facings

Turn body and sleeves with WS facing. With smaller circ
needle and RS of cut edge facing, pick up same number
of sts along cut edges of armholes, picking up sts in
same spaces as sleeve sts.

Working back and forth, beg with a WS row and work 5
rows of St st. Bind off loosely.

Fold facing toward body, covering cut edge, then sew
loosely to WS. Make facing along rem armhole to match.

COLLAR

Cut open front neck opening.

With smaller circ needle and RS facing, beg at lower-right
edge of front neck opening and pick up and k140 (144,
144, 148, 148, 152) sts along front and back neck edges;
do not pick up sts along bound-off sts at bottom of
front neck opening.

Working back and forth, beg with a WS row and set rib in
this manner: p3, *k2, p2; rep from * to last 3 sts, end p3.

Next row, k3 *p2, k2; rep from * to last 3 sts, end k3. Rep
last 2 rows until collar measures approx $2\frac{1}{4}$" (5.5cm).

Next row, dec 1 st at beg and end of row—138 (142, 142,
146, 146, 150) sts. Work even until collar measures $5\frac{1}{2}$"
(14cm). Bind off loosely in rib.

Neatly sew edges of rib to bottom of front opening, having
both sides of collar meet at center of opening.

FRONT NECK FACINGS

Turn body with WS facing. With smaller circ needle and RS
of cut edge facing, pick up same number of sts along
cut edges of front neck edge, picking up sts in same
spaces as collar sts.

Working back and forth, beg with a WS row and work 5
rows of St st. Bind off loosely.

Fold facing toward body, covering cut edge, then sew
loosely to WS. Make facing along rem side of front neck
edge to match.

Men's Sweaters

Sizes
S (M, L, XL, XXL)
Sample size is Medium

Measurements
Chest: 41 (45, 49, 53, 57)"/104 (114.5, 124.5, 134.5, 145)cm
Body Length: 26 (26$^1/_2$, 27, 27$^1/_2$, 28)"/66 (67.5, 68.5, 70, 71)cm
Sleeve Length: 21$^3/_4$" (55cm) all sizes

Yarn
Heilo by Dale of Norway (100% pure Norwegian wool, 109 yd. [100m]/1$^3/_4$ oz. [50g])
12 (13, 14, 16, 17) balls, color #2931 Light Sheep Heather (MC)
3 (4, 4, 5, 5) balls, color #2671 Dark Taupe (CC1)
1 (1, 1, 1, 1) ball, color #4246 Wine (CC2)
1 (1, 1, 1, 1) ball, color #5744 Norwegian Blue (CC3)
1 (2, 2, 2, 3) ball(s), color #9145 Asparagus (CC4)

Needles and Notions
1 each U.S. size 2 and 3, or 4 (2.75mm and 3mm, or 3.5mm) circular needles, or size needed to obtain gauge
1 set each U.S. size 2 and 3, or 4 (2.75mm and 3mm, or 3.5mm) double-pointed needles, or size needed to obtain gauge
Crochet hook U.S. size B-1 (2.25mm)
Stitch markers
Stitch holders—optional
Contrasting sewing thread
Matching sewing thread
Zipper 6$^1/_4$" (16cm)
Facing 13$^1/_2$" (34.5cm)—optional

Gauge
24 sts and 28 rnds over colorwork pattern using larger needle = 4" (10cm)

➤ Take time to check your gauge.

Heilo Pullover
DALE DESIGN

Here's a classic Norwegian ski sweater reinterpreted in an updated color combination while still retaining details you would expect to find. It looks good not only on the ski slopes but anywhere you need a sweater, whether you wear it indoors or out.

Though it's sized here for men, don't be afraid to knit it for yourself in feminine colors. Change the zip placket to buttons and loops to complete the look.

DIRECTIONS
BODY
With smaller circ needle and MC, CO 246 (270, 294, 318, 342) sts. Join and, working in the rnd, make sure sts are not twisted. Mark beg of rnd.

Work 2" (5cm) of k1, p1 rib.

Change to larger circ needle and place side markers at the beg of rnd and after 123 (135, 147, 159, 171) sts.

Work Pattern I (page 120). Beg Main Pattern as shown on chart and work to side marker, then beg again at right-hand side of chart as before and work to end of rnd. Cont 6-rnd rep until body measures approx 15$^1/_2$ (16, 16$^1/_2$, 17, 17$^1/_2$)"/39.5 (40.5, 42, 43, 44.5)cm from bottom of rib, ending with rnd 3 or 6 of rep.

Beg Pattern II in same manner as Main Pattern, and work until body measures 18$^1/_2$ (19, 19$^1/_2$, 20, 20$^1/_2$)"/47 (48.5, 49.5, 51, 52)cm from bottom of rib.

PLACKET OPENING
Next rnd, work first 60 (66, 72, 78, 84) sts as est, bind off the next 3 sts for placket opening, then work to end of rnd—243 (267, 291, 315, 339) sts. CO 3 new sts over bound-off sts of previous rnd (these are cutting sts; work in background color throughout and exclude from pattern and st counts; if only one color is used in a rnd, work with the color only and do not strand the MC). Work until body measures 23$^1/_4$ (23$^3/_4$, 24, 24$^1/_2$, 25)"/59 (60.5, 61, 62, 63.5)cm from bottom of rib.

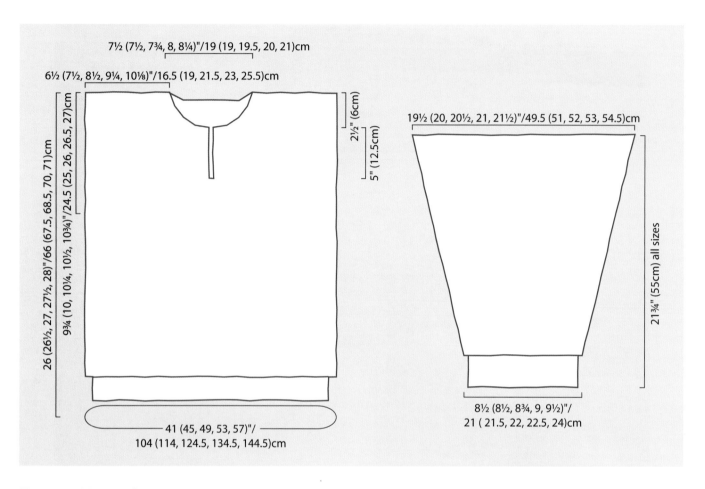

7½ (7½, 7¾, 8, 8¼)"/19 (19, 19.5, 20, 21)cm

6½ (7½, 8½, 9¼, 10⅛)"/16.5 (19, 21.5, 23, 25.5)cm

2½" (6cm)

5" (12.5cm)

26 (26½, 27, 27½, 28)"/66 (67.5, 68.5, 70, 71)cm

9¾ (10, 10¼, 10½, 10¾)"/24.5 (25, 26, 26.5, 27)cm

41 (45, 49, 53, 57)"/
104 (114, 124.5, 134.5, 144.5)cm

19½ (20, 20½, 21, 21½)"/49.5 (51, 52, 53, 54.5)cm

21¾" (55cm) all sizes

8½ (8½, 8¾, 9, 9½)"/
21 (21.5, 22, 22.5, 24)cm

FRONT NECK OPENING

Work first 55 (60, 65, 70, 75) sts as est, bind off the next 13 (15, 17, 19, 21) sts for front neck opening (the 3 cutting sts, plus 5 [6, 7, 8, 9] sts on either side), then work to end of rnd—233 (255, 277, 299, 321) sts. Cut yarn and slip left front shoulder sts from left needle to right needle. Reattach yarn and, working back and forth, beg rows at front neck edges. Cont pattern and bind off 4 sts at the beg of first 2 rows, 3 sts at the beg of next 2 rows, 2 sts at the beg of next 4 rows, then dec 1 st at the beg and end of every other row 4 times. **At the same time,** when body measures 25¼ (25¾, 26¼, 26¾, 27¼)"/64 (65.5, 66.5, 68, 69)cm, shape back neck opening.

BACK NECK OPENING

Next row, cont front neck shaping and work front sts and first 45 (50, 55, 60, 65) sts of back. Bind off the next 33 (35, 37, 39, 41) sts for back neck opening, then work to end of row. Working each side of body separately over both front and back of each shoulder, complete pattern and bind off every other row at back neck edge, 3 sts once, then 2 sts once—80 (90, 100, 110, 120) sts. When pattern is complete, knit 1 row on WS (or purl 1 row on RS), then bind off. Complete other side of body to match.

SLEEVES

With smaller dpns and MC, CO 52 (54, 56, 58, 60) sts. Join and, working in the rnd, mark beg of rnd.

Work 2" (5cm) of k1, p1 rib and inc 11 (13, 15, 17, 19) sts evenly spaced across last rnd—63 (67, 71, 75, 79) sts.

Change to larger dpns. Work Pattern I, placing center st of pattern at center of rnd. **At the same time,** inc 1 st at the beg and end of every 5th rnd 16 (18, 18, 25, 25) times, then every 4th rnd 13 (10, 10, 2, 2) times, leaving 2 sts between inc sts and working inc sts into pattern.

In the meantime, when Pattern I is complete, beg Main Pattern, placing center st of chart at center of sleeve and cont inc as set—121 (123, 127, 129, 133) sts.

When sleeve measures approx 17½" (44.5cm) from bottom of rib, end Main Pattern with a rnd 3 or 6 of rep. Work Pattern III and cont rem inc.

Knit 1 rnd with CC4. Purl 5 rnds for facing and, **at the same time,** inc 1 st at the beg and end of first rnd, then every other rnd twice more—127 (129, 133, 135, 139) sts. Bind off loosely. *Optional:* If desired, change back to MC after 1st rnd of facing.

Make second sleeve to match.

FINISHING

Block pieces to finished measurements; do not block ribs. *Optional:* Wet blocking works with this yarn.

Measure sleeves for armhole depth and mark on each side of the body, from purl rnd before bound-off edge at shoulders down for armhole openings.

Sew 2 rows of machine stitching, 2 sts out from where markers were placed and across the bottom of the 4 sts for armholes. Cut open the armholes.

Sew shoulders tog using whip st, and working from RS.

NECKBAND

With smaller circ needle, MC and with RS facing, pick up and k119 (121, 123, 125, 127) sts along neck edge using a crochet hook to pick up sts kwise.

Working back and forth, beg with a WS row and work 14 rows of k1, p1 rib.

Knit 1 row on WS for fold line.

Work 5 rows of rib. Change to CC4 and purl 1 row. Work 1 row of rib. Change to CC3 and purl 1 row. Work 1 row of rib. Change to CC1 and purl 1 row. Work 1 row of rib. Change to MC and purl 1 row. Work 2 rows of rib. Bind off loosely in rib.

FRONT PLACKETS

With smaller circ or dpns, MC and with RS facing, pick up and k12 sts per 2" (5cm) along right front opening edge from bottom of placket opening to neckband fold line in same manner as neckband.

Working back and forth, beg with a WS row and work 4 rows of St st. Purl 1 row on RS for fold line, then work 3 rows of St st. Bind off neatly. *Optional:* Do not bind off but slip sts to st holder.

Work placket on rem side of front opening and end of neckband to match.

Neatly trim loose ends along cut edges. Turn plackets to inside along fold lines, covering cut edges, then neatly sew to WS. Neatly sew top edges of plackets closed. Neatly sew lower edges of plackets to bottom of placket opening, with fold lines meeting at center of opening. If sts were slipped to st holders, fold placket over cut edge and graft sts to pick up row along WS using Kitchner st.

ZIPPER

Pin zipper into placket opening.

NOTE

If using a facing behind zipper, baste half of facing to back of each side of zipper tape, with edges meeting at center under zipper. Neatly sew zipper to body by hand or machine. If sewing zipper in by machine, sew along sides of zipper only.

Fold neckband to inside along fold line, making sure zipper can move easily past ends of neckband. Neatly sew neckband to WS, and ends of neckband to edge of placket.

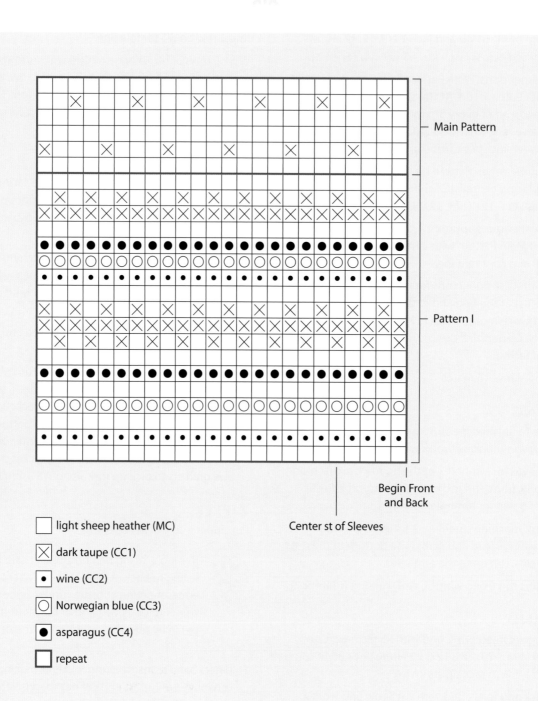

Main Pattern

Pattern I

Begin Front
and Back

Center st of Sleeves

☐ light sheep heather (MC)

☒ dark taupe (CC1)

⊡ wine (CC2)

◯ Norwegian blue (CC3)

● asparagus (CC4)

☐ repeat

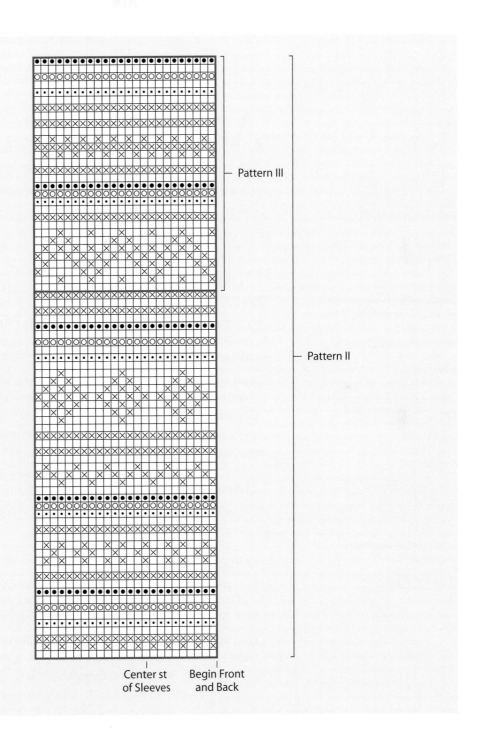

Pattern III

Pattern II

Center st
of Sleeves

Begin Front
and Back

Oak Vest

Sizes
S (M, L, XL, XXL)
Sample size is Medium

Measurements
Chest: 39 (43, 47, 51, 55)"/99 (109, 119.5,
   129.5, 139.5)cm
Length: 24 (24³/₄, 25¹/₂, 26, 27)"/61 (63, 65,
   66, 68.5)cm
Armhole: 9¹/₄ (9¹/₂, 9³/₄, 10, 10¹/₄)"/23.5
   (24, 25, 25.5, 26)cm

Yarn
Oak by Fibranatura (60% superwash
   merino wool/20% linen/20% silk, 175 yd.
   [160m]/1 ³/₄ oz. [50g])
6 (7, 7, 8, 8) balls, color #40206 Pewter

Needles and Notions
1 each U.S. size 5 and 6 (3.75mm and
   4mm) circular needles, or size needed to
   obtain gauge
Cable needle
Stitch holders
Stitch markers
Contrasting sewing thread
6 (6, 7, 7, 7) buttons, ³/₄" (19mm)—JHB
   International, #90880 Calvin

Gauge
28 sts and 28 rnds over pattern using
   larger needles = 4" (10cm)

➤ Take time to check your gauge.

Almost everyone likes a cable and ribbed vest of one form or another. This classic form gets better than usual treatment in this design. The construction techniques used for the front opening, neck and armholes demonstrate how well the Norwegian method works—no unsightly cut edges to fray on the inside and rib bands on the outside that don't look like stuffed sausages.

DIRECTIONS

BODY

With smaller circ needle, CO 257 (287, 309, 337, 363) sts. Working back and forth, beg with a RS row and work 1" (2.5cm) of k1, p1 rib and dec 1 st on last row; end with a WS row—256 (286, 308, 336, 362) sts.

Change to larger circ needle and place side markers 62 (70, 75, 82, 89) sts from beg and end of row. With RS facing, CO 4 new sts at end of row (these are cutting sts; work in St st throughout and exclude from st counts). Join and, working in the rnd, mark beg of rnd and beg rnds at center front at center of cutting sts.

Next rnd, knit cutting sts, beg at right-hand side of chart (page 126) as marked for right front, and work to side marker, beg as shown for back and work to next side marker, beg as shown for left front, then work to end of rnd.

Cont working as est until body measures 14³/₄ (15¹/₄, 15³/₄, 16, 16³/₄)"/37.5 (38.5, 40, 40.5, 42.5)cm from bottom of rib.

ARMHOLES

Next rnd, work cutting sts and next 58 (64, 67, 72, 77) sts, bind off the next 8 (12, 16, 20, 24) sts for armhole, work next 124 (134, 142, 152, 160) sts, bind off the next 8 (12, 16, 20, 24) sts for armhole, then work to end of rnd—240 (262, 276, 296, 314) sts.

CO 4 cutting sts over each armhole, cont working in the rnd, and dec 1 st before and after armhole, cutting sts every rnd 0 (0, 0, 3, 5) times, then every other rnd 8 (10, 10, 10, 10) times. **At the same time,** when body measures 15¹/₂ (15³/₄, 16¹/₂, 16¹/₂, 17¹/₂)"/39.5 (40, 42, 42, 44.5)cm from bottom of rib, beg shaping front neck opening.

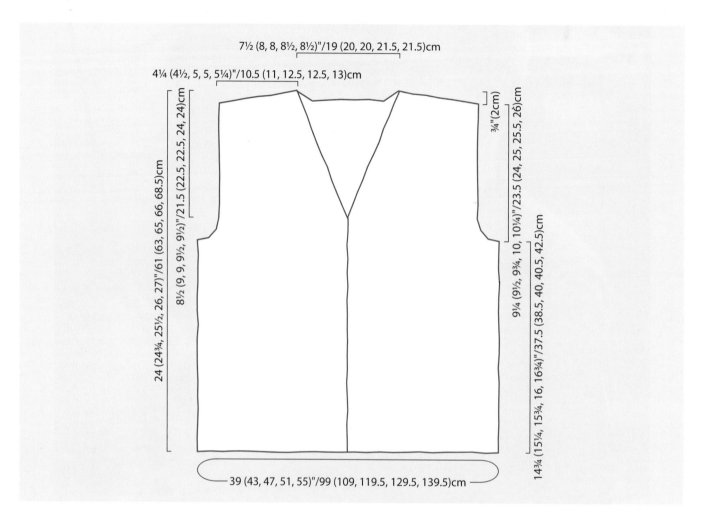

7½ (8, 8, 8½, 8½)"/19 (20, 20, 21.5, 21.5)cm

4¼ (4½, 5, 5, 5¼)"/10.5 (11, 12.5, 12.5, 13)cm

¾"(2cm)

24 (24¾, 25½, 26, 27)"/61 (63, 65, 66, 68.5)cm

8½ (9, 9, 9½, 9½)"/21.5 (22.5, 22.5, 24, 24)cm

9¼ (9½, 9¾, 10, 10¼)"/23.5 (24, 25, 25.5, 26)cm

14¾ (15¼, 15¾, 16, 16¾)"/37.5 (38.5, 40, 40.5, 42.5)cm

39 (43, 47, 51, 55)"/99 (109, 119.5, 129.5, 139.5)cm

FRONT NECK OPENING

Dec 1 st, 2 sts in from cutting sts at beg and end of rnd, alternating every 2nd, then 3rd rnd 10 (11, 10, 11, 11) times (20 [22, 20, 22, 22] sts dec on each side of front), then every 3rd rnd 0 (0, 1, 0, 1) times, working dec at beg of rnd as ssk, and at end of rnd k2tog—168 (178, 194, 200, 208) sts.

Work even until armhole measures 9¹/₄ (9¹/₂, 9³/₄, 10, 10¹/₄)"/ 23.5 (24, 25, 25.5, 26)cm, ending with an even number rnd of rep, and bind off armhole cutting sts on last rnd.

FRONT SHOULDER SHAPING

Cut yarn and slip left front shoulder sts from right needle to left needle. Reattach yarn and, working back and forth, cont with a RS row and work 54 (56, 64, 66, 69) sts (the first 30 [31, 36, 37, 39] sts, the 4 cutting sts, then 20 [21, 24, 25, 26] sts), bring yarn to RS, wrap next st, then turn. Slip first st and tighten it slightly, work next 44 (46, 52, 53, 56) sts, wrap next st, then turn. Slip first st and tighten it slightly, work next 34 (36, 40, 41, 43) sts, then turn. Slip first st and tighten it slightly, work next 10 (11, 12, 13, 13) sts, bind off the cutting sts, then work next 10 (11, 12, 13, 13) sts. Slip sts for both shoulders to st holders.

BACK NECK AND SHOULDER SHAPING

Working back and forth, beg with a RS row. Work 35 (36, 41, 42, 44) sts, bind off the next 38 (44, 42, 42, 44) sts for neck opening and dec 2 sts over each cable, then work 26 sts, wrap next st and turn.

Working each side of back separately, shape shoulders same as front and bind off every other row at neck edge, 3 sts once, then 2 sts once. Slip rem 30 (31, 36, 37, 39) sts to st holder. Complete other side of back to match, placing neck and shoulder shaping on opposite sides.

FINISHING

Sew 2 rows of machine stitching along both sides of cutting sts for front and armhole openings. Cut open sts along front opening.

Block body to finished measurements.

Cut open armholes. Slip sts from holders to larger circ needle, with neck edges at ends of needle. Bind off using a two-needle method with live sts on both needles, making sure to work wraps tog with the sts they wrap.

ARMHOLE FACINGS

With smaller circ needle and RS facing, beg at bottom of armhole and pick up and k97 (99, 101, 103, 105) sts along one armhole edge. Join and, working in the rnd, mark beg of rnd.

Knit 1 rnd, then purl 1 rnd for fold line.

Beg working back and forth, work 6 rows of St st and dec 1 st at the beg and end of every row. Bind off loosely.

Fold facing to inside along fold line, covering cut edges, and sew loosely to WS.

Work facing along rem armhole.

ARMHOLE RIBS

With smaller circ needle and RS facing, beg at bottom of armhole and pick up and k1 st in each upper p-loop along fold edge (lower p-loop will show on RS). Join and, working in the rnd, mark beg of rnd.

Work 3 rnds of k1, p1 rib and dec 1 st on 1st rnd—96 (98, 100, 102, 104) sts. Bind off loosely in rib.

Work rib along rem armhole.

NECK FACING

With smaller circ needle and RS facing, beg at bottom of right front and pick up and k10 sts per 2" (5cm) along front edge, 40 (42, 42, 44, 44) sts across back neck edge, then 10 sts per 2" (5cm) along left front edge.

Working back and forth, beg with a WS row and purl 1 row. Purl 1 row for fold line. Work 6 rows of St st, then bind off loosely. Fold facing to inside along fold line, covering cut edges, then neatly sew facing to WS.

Mark placement for buttons on both sides of front facing, placing top button at beg of front neck shaping, bottom button approx 1/2" (1.5cm) from bottom edge, then evenly space rem buttons in between.

NECK RIB

With smaller circ needle and RS facing, beg at bottom of right front and pick up and k1 st in each upper p-loop along fold edge along right front, around back neck and down left front.

Working back and forth, beg with a WS row and work 2 rows of k1, p1 rib.

Next row, work buttonholes on left front, each over 3 sts as marked. Work buttonholes by binding off 3 sts, then on next row CO 3 new sts over bound-off sts of previous row.

Cont working until 7 rows of rib have been worked. Bind off loosely in rib.

Sew buttons to right front rib as marked.

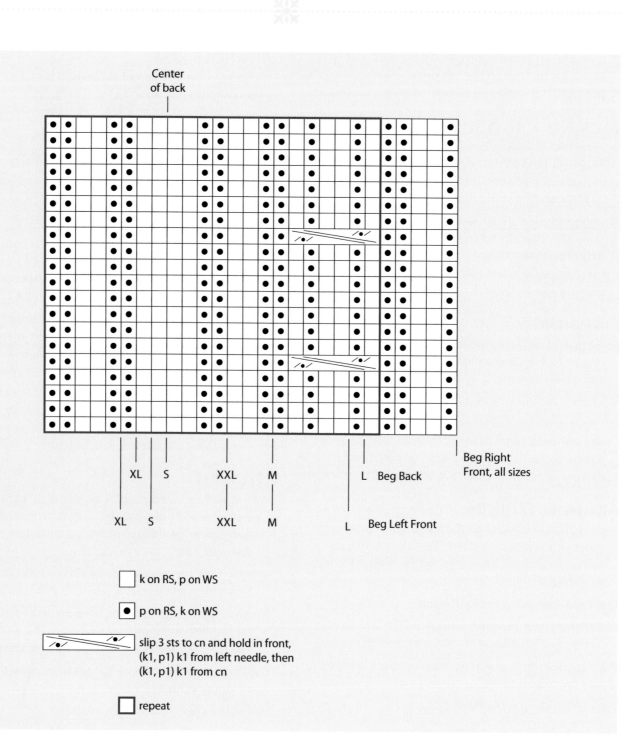

Center
of back

XL   S   XXL   M   L   Beg Back

XL   S   XXL   M   L   Beg Left Front

Beg Right
Front, all sizes

k on RS, p on WS

● p on RS, k on WS

slip 3 sts to cn and hold in front,
(k1, p1) k1 from left needle, then
(k1, p1) k1 from cn

repeat

Cotton Jeans Henley

Every man needs a casual pullover such as this one. It's perfect for cooler summer evenings or while enjoying the day at the beach or on the lake. Quick and easy to work in the round, the twill tape used to face the cut edges of this design keep bulky seams to a minimum. What could be better than that?

DIRECTIONS

BODY

With circ needle, CO 184 (204, 224, 244, 260) sts. Join and, working in the rnd, make sure sts are not twisted. Mark beg of rnd and place side markers at the beg of rnd and after 92 (102, 112, 122, 130) sts.

*Purl 1 rnd, knit 1 rnd; rep from * once more, then purl 1 rnd.

Beg St st and work until body measures $16\frac{1}{2}$ ($16\frac{1}{2}$, 17, 17, 17)"/42 (42, 43, 43, 43)cm from bottom edge, ending last rnd 3 (3, 4, 4, 5) sts before end of rnd.

ARMHOLES

Bind off the next 6 (6, 8, 8, 10) sts for armhole, knit to 3 (3, 4, 4, 5) sts before next marker, bind off the next 6 (6, 8, 8, 10) sts for armhole, then knit to end of rnd—172 (192, 208, 228, 240) sts. Next rnd, CO 4 new sts over bound-off sts of previous rnd (these are cutting sts; work in St st throughout and exclude from st counts). Cont working in the rnd and, **at the same time,** dec 1 st on each side of the cutting sts every other rnd 3 (6, 7, 9, 10) times, working dec before markers as k2tog, and after markers as ssk. **At the same time,** when body measures $17\frac{3}{4}$ (18, 19, $19\frac{1}{4}$, $19\frac{3}{4}$)"/45 (45.5, 48.5, 49, 50)cm from bottom edge, beg placket opening.

PLACKET OPENING

Bind off the center 4 sts of front for placket opening—156 (164, 176, 188, 196) sts. CO 4 new sts over bound-off sts of previous rnd and cont St st until body measures $19\frac{1}{2}$ ($19\frac{1}{2}$, 20, $20\frac{1}{2}$, $20\frac{1}{2}$)"/49.5 (49.5, 51, 52, 52)cm from bottom edge. Work Arrow Pattern, beg as shown (page 131), and work to side marker, beg again at right-hand side of chart as before, then work to end of rnd.

Sizes
S (M, L, XL, XXL)
Sample size is Medium

Measurements
Chest: 39 (43, 47, 51, 55)"/99 (109, 119.5, 129.5, 139.5)cm
Body Length: $25\frac{1}{2}$ (26, 27, $27\frac{1}{2}$, 28)"/65 (66, 68.5, 70, 71)cm
Sleeve Length to Underarm: 22" (56cm) for all sizes

Yarn
Cotton Jeans by Rowan Classic Yarns (100% cotton, 82 yd. [75m]/$1\frac{3}{4}$ oz. [50g]) 17 (19, 21, 23, 25) balls, color #366 Blue Jeans

Needles
1 each U.S. size 6 (4mm) circular needles, or size needed to obtain gauge
1 set of 5 U.S. size 6 (4mm) double-pointed needles
Cable needle
Stitch holders
Stitch markers
3 buttons $\frac{3}{4}$" (19mm)—La Mode, #26302
2 yd. (2m) wide twill tape, braid, or ribbon $\frac{5}{8}$"–$\frac{3}{4}$" (16mm–20mm)

Gauge
19 sts and 26 rows over St st; 22 sts over cable pattern = 4" (10cm)

➤ Take time to check your gauge.

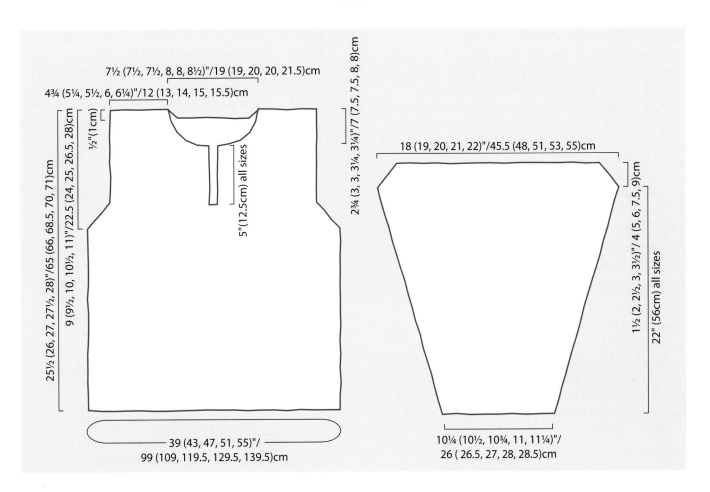

7½ (7½, 7½, 8, 8, 8½)"/19 (19, 20, 20, 21.5)cm

4¾ (5¼, 5½, 6, 6¼)"/12 (13, 14, 15, 15.5)cm

½"(1cm)

25½ (26, 27, 27½, 28)"/65 (66, 68.5, 70, 71)cm

9 (9½, 10, 10½, 11)"/22.5 (24, 25, 26.5, 28)cm

5"(12.5cm) all sizes

2¾ (3, 3¼, 3¼)"/7 (7.5, 7.5, 8, 8)cm

39 (43, 47, 51, 55)"/
99 (109, 119.5, 129.5, 139.5)cm

18 (19, 20, 21, 22)"/45.5 (48, 51, 53, 55)cm

1½ (2, 2½, 3, 3½)"/ 4 (5, 6, 7.5, 9)cm

22" (56cm) all sizes

10¼ (10½, 10¾, 11, 11¼)"/
26 (26.5, 27, 28, 28.5)cm

Knit 1 rnd and inc 7 sts evenly spaced across each half of front, and 14 sts evenly spaced across back (do not inc within the cutting sts)—184 (192, 204, 216, 224) sts. Beg Cable Pattern as shown and work to marker (working 4 placket cutting sts in St st), then beg again as shown and work to end of rnd.

NOTE If a complete cable cannot be worked at side edges, work those sts in St st.

Cont as est until body measures 22¾ (23, 24, 24¼, 24¾)"/ 58 (58.5, 61, 61.5, 63)cm from bottom edge, ending with an even number rnd of pattern.

FRONT NECK OPENING

Next rnd, work cutting sts and first 39 (41, 42, 45, 46) sts as est, bind off the next 16 (16, 20, 20, 22) sts for front neck opening (the 4 cutting sts, plus 6 [6, 8, 8, 9] sts on each side), then work to end of rnd—172 (180, 188, 200, 206) sts. Cut yarn and slip left front shoulder sts from left needle to right needle. Reattach yarn and, working back and forth, beg rows at front neck edges.

Beg with a WS row and bind off 4 sts at the beg of first 2 rows, 3 sts at the beg of next 2 rows, 2 sts at the beg of next 2 rows. Dec 1 st at the beg and end of every other row twice, then every 4th row once—148 (156, 164, 176, 182) sts. Work even until body measures approx 25 (25½, 26½, 27, 27½)"/63.5 (65, 67.5, 68.5, 70)cm from bottom edge.

BACK NECK OPENING

Next row, work front and cutting sts, then first 30 (32, 33, 36, 37) sts of back, bind off the next 34 (34, 38, 38, 40) sts for back neck opening, then work to end of row. Working each side of body separately over front and back of each shoulder, cont pattern and bind off every other row at back neck edge, 3 sts once—54 (58, 60, 66, 68) sts. Work 1 row, dec 1 st over each cable, and bind off armhole cutting sts. Slip rem sts to holders. Complete other side of body to match.

SLEEVES

With dpns, CO 46 (48, 50, 52, 54) sts. Join and, working in the rnd, make sure sts are not twisted. Mark beg of rnd.

*Purl 1 rnd, knit 1 rnd; rep from * once more, then purl 1 rnd.

Beg St st and, **at the same time,** inc 1 st at the beg and end of rnd, every 6th rnd 0 (0, 12, 19, 25) times, every 7th rnd 10 (21, 11, 5, 0) times, then every 8th rnd 10 (0, 0, 0, 0) times, leaving 2 sts between inc sts—86 (90, 96, 100, 104) sts. Work even until sleeve measures approx 21½" (54.5cm) from bottom edge, work first 4 rnds of Arrow Pattern, ending last rnd 3 (3, 4, 4, 5) sts before end of rnd.

Sleeve Cap

Bind off the next 6 (6, 8, 8, 10) sts, then work to end of rnd—80 (84, 88, 92, 94) sts. Working back and forth, cont pattern and dec 1 st at the beg and end of every RS row 6 times—68 (72, 76, 80, 82) sts. Work 1 more row. Bind off.

Make second sleeve to match.

FINISHING

Block pieces to finished measurements; wet blocking works well with this yarn.

Sew 2 rows of machine stitching along each side of armhole and placket cutting sts. Cut open placket opening and armholes.

With WS held tog, slip sts for front and back of one shoulder to circ needle, alternating 1 st from front, then 1 st from back. Pass second st on left needle over first st and off needle, k first st—1 st on right needle. *Rep once more—2 sts on left needle. Pass first st on right needle over second st to bind off—1 st rem on right needle. Rep from * to end of row. Fasten off. Rep with rem shoulder.

NECKBAND

With circ needle and RS facing, pick up and k72 (76, 78, 80, 82) sts along right front, back, and left front neck edge. Working back and forth, beg with a WS row and knit 4 rows. Bind off kwise.

BUTTON PLACKET

With circ needles or dpns and RS facing, pick up and k31 sts along right opening edge, 1 st in from machine stitching, working from bottom of opening to top of neckband. Working back and forth, beg with a WS row and knit 3 rows. Work 4 rows of St st. Bind off kwise.

Mark placement for buttons, placing top button at neck line, then evenly space rem 2 buttons along placket.

BUTTONHOLE PLACKET

With circ needles or dpns and RS facing, pick up and k31 sts along left-opening edge. Working back and forth, beg with a WS row and knit 6 rows. **At the same time,** on 4th row, work buttonholes, each over 2 sts as marked. Bind off neatly kwise. Sew buttons to button placket as marked.

Pin sleeves into armholes, placing centers of sleeves at shoulder seams. Sew sleeves to body using whip st or combined whip st/mattress st. Cut 2 pieces of twill tape to cover cut edges of armhole openings, plus approx 1" (2.5cm). With cut edges folded toward body, pin tape to cut edges along each armhole and turn under ends. Neatly sew tape to body along all edges. Cut 2 pieces of twill tape to cover cut edges of placket opening, plus approx 1" (2.5cm). With cut edges folded toward body, pin tape to cut edges of placket opening, and turn under ends of tape. Neatly sew tape to body along all edges.

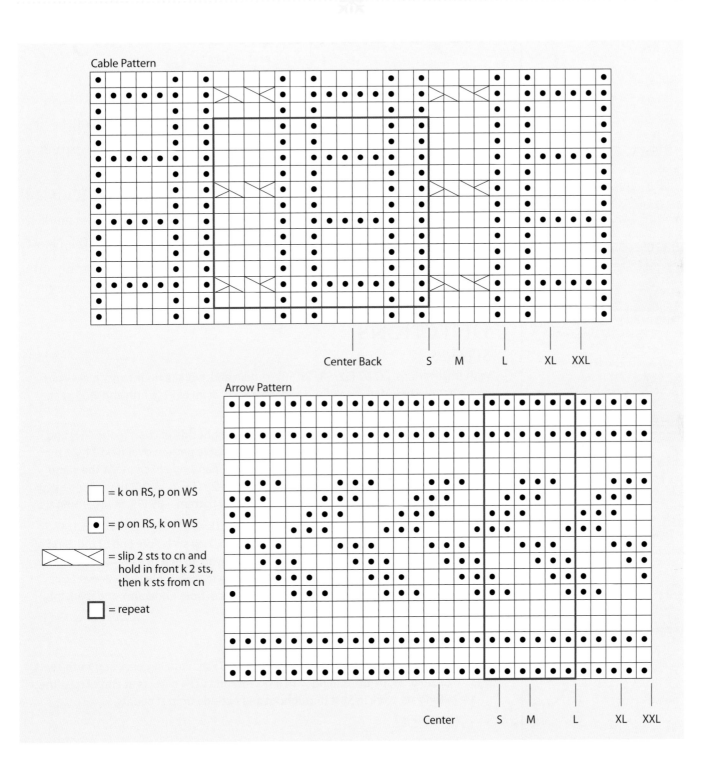

Cable Pattern

Center Back   S   M   L   XL   XXL

Arrow Pattern

= k on RS, p on WS

= p on RS, k on WS

= slip 2 sts to cn and hold in front k 2 sts, then k sts from cn

= repeat

Center   S   M   L   XL   XXL

Royal Llama Linen Cardigan

Sizes
S (M, L, XL, XXL)
Sample size is Medium

Measurements
Chest: 39 (44, 49, 54$\frac{1}{2}$, 59$\frac{3}{4}$)"/ 99 (112, 124.5, 138.5, 152)cm
Body Length: 26 (26$\frac{1}{2}$, 27$\frac{1}{2}$, 28, 29)"/ 66 (67.5, 70, 71, 73.5)cm
Sleeve Length to Underarm: 17$\frac{1}{2}$ (17$\frac{1}{2}$, 18$\frac{1}{4}$, 18$\frac{3}{4}$, 19$\frac{3}{4}$)"/ 44.5 (44.5, 46.5, 47.5, 50)cm

Yarn
Royal Llama Linen by Plymouth Yarns (40% fine llama/35% silk/25% linen, 109 yd. [100m]/1 $\frac{3}{4}$ oz [50g])
11 (13, 14, 16, 17) skeins, color #1542 Camel

Needles
1 set each U.S. size 5 and 6 (3.75mm and 4mm) circular needles, or size needed to obtain gauge
1 set each U.S. size 5 and 6 (3.75mm and 4mm) double-pointed needles, or size needed to obtain gauge
Cable needle
Stitch markers
5 buttons, $\frac{3}{4}$" (19mm)—JHB International, #93282 Rusticana

Gauge
21 sts and 29 rows over pattern = 4" (10cm)

➤ Take time to check your gauge.

Casual and very comfortable, this classic raglan design will be the sweater he'll want to wear all the time. He may find you wearing it too, so make a second one for yourself.

The sleeves are worked first, then added to the body, which is worked in the round. The yoke is continued in the round for the raglan armholes, while also decreasing for the V-neck. Facings at the front edges keep most of the bulk away from the center so the button bands move smoothly into the shawl collar.

DIRECTIONS

SLEEVES
With smaller dpns, CO 52 (52, 58, 58, 58) sts. Join and, working in the rnd, make sure sts are not twisted. Mark beg of rnd and work 1$\frac{1}{4}$" (3cm) of k1, p1 rib and inc 1 st at center of last rnd—53 (53, 59, 59, 59) sts.

Set pattern across next rnd in this manner: Beg at right side of chart (page 135) and work first 21 (21, 24, 24, 24) sts as shown, work cable pattern over next 11 sts, then work rem 21 (21, 24, 24, 24) sts as shown on left-hand side of chart. **At the same time,** inc 1 st at the beg and end of every 5th rnd 0 (15, 2, 18, 20) times, then every 6th rnd 18 (6, 18, 5, 5) times, working inc sts into pattern—89 (95, 99, 105, 109) sts.

Work even until sleeve measures 17$\frac{1}{2}$ (17$\frac{1}{2}$, 18$\frac{1}{4}$, 18$\frac{3}{4}$, 19$\frac{3}{4}$)"/44.5 (44.5, 46.5, 47.5, 50)cm from bottom of rib, ending last rnd 4 (5, 6, 7, 8) sts before end of rnd. Bind off the next 7 (9, 11, 13, 15) sts for underarm, then work to end of rnd—82 (86, 88, 92, 94) sts. Set sleeve aside and make second sleeve to match. Measure sleeve 14$\frac{1}{4}$ (14$\frac{1}{4}$, 14$\frac{3}{4}$, 14$\frac{3}{4}$, 15$\frac{1}{4}$)"/36 (36, 37.5, 37.5, 38.5)cm from underarm, and mark this rnd; pattern on body will beg here.

BODY
With smaller circ needle, CO 205 (233, 261, 289, 317) sts. Working back and forth, work 1$\frac{1}{4}$" (3cm) of k1, p1 rib, ending with a WS row and CO 4 new sts at end of row (these are cutting sts; work in St st throughout and exclude from st counts).

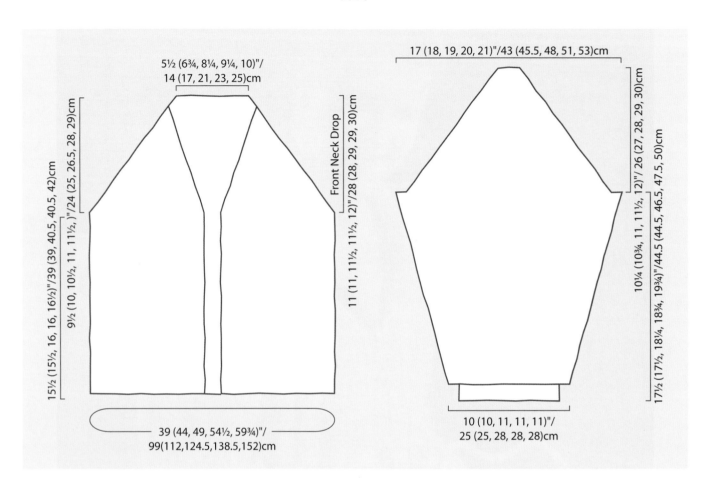

5½ (6¾, 8¼, 9¼, 10)"/
14 (17, 21, 23, 25)cm

15½ (15½, 16, 16, 16½)"/39 (39, 40.5, 40.5, 42)cm

9½ (10, 10½, 11, 11½,)"/24 (25, 26.5, 28, 29)cm

Front Neck Drop

11 (11, 11½, 11½, 12)"/28 (28, 29, 29, 30)cm

39 (44, 49, 54½, 59¾)"/
99(112,124.5,138.5,152)cm

17 (18, 19, 20, 21)"/43 (45.5, 48, 51, 53)cm

10¼ (10¾, 11, 11½, 12)"/ 26 (27, 28, 29, 30)cm

17½ (17½, 18¼, 18¾, 19¾)"/44.5 (44.5, 46.5, 47.5, 50)cm

10 (10, 11, 11, 11)"/
25 (25, 28, 28, 28)cm

Join and, working in the rnd, mark beg of rnd and beg rnds at center of cutting sts. Change to larger circ needle and place side markers 51 (58, 65, 72, 79) sts out from both sides of cutting sts (103 [117, 131, 145, 159] sts for back).

Beg with same pattern rnd as marked on sleeves and set pattern across 1st rnd in this manner: knit cutting sts, beg Main Pattern as shown for right front and work to side st, beg back as shown and work to next side marker, beg at right-hand side of chart and work side st, then work to end rnd. Cont as est until body measures 15½ (15½, 16, 16, 16½)"/39 (39, 40.5, 40.5, 42)cm from bottom of rib and end with same rnd of rep as sleeves before armhole.

Next rnd, work to 3 (4, 5, 6, 7) sts before side st, bind off the next 7 (9, 11, 12, 15) sts for armhole, work to 3 (4, 5, 6, 7) sts before next side st, bind off the next 7 (9, 11, 12, 15) sts for armhole, then work to end of rnd—191 (215, 239, 265, 287) sts.

Yoke

With RS facing, slip sts for all pieces to larger circ needle in this order: front, sleeve, back, then sleeve, and place markers where pieces meet—355 (387, 415, 449, 475) sts. Adjust sts on needle so that rnds will beg at center front.

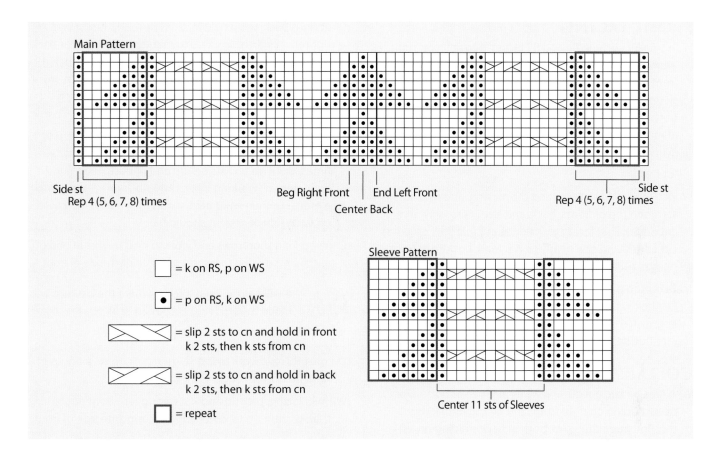

Main Pattern

Side st
Rep 4 (5, 6, 7, 8) times

Beg Right Front | End Left Front
Center Back

Side st
Rep 4 (5, 6, 7, 8) times

☐ = k on RS, p on WS

● = p on RS, k on WS

⧖ = slip 2 sts to cn and hold in front k 2 sts, then k sts from cn

⧗ = slip 2 sts to cn and hold in back k 2 sts, then k sts from cn

☐ = repeat

Sleeve Pattern

Center 11 sts of Sleeves

Next rnd, *work to 2 sts before armhole marker, k2tog, ssk; rep from * 3 more times, then work to end of rnd—8 sts dec. Work 1 rnd without shaping armholes. Cont dec at armholes on next rnd, then every other rnd 30 (32, 34, 36, 39) more times.

At the same time, dec 1 st, 1 st in on body side from cutting sts at front opening on 1st rnd, then every 4th rnd 14 (16, 17, 18, 20) more times, working dec as p2tog or k2tog according to pattern to shape front neck edge—69 (81, 99, 107, 105) sts.

Work 3 (5, 5, 6, 6) more rnds, working 2 (3, 3, 4, 4) more raglan dec on back, 2 (3, 3, 3, 0) more dec on sleeves, and 0 (0, 3, 4, 4) more raglan dec on each side of front—57 (63, 75, 79, 89) sts.

Bind off and dec 1 st over each cable on sleeves.

FINISHING

Sew body and sleeves tog at underarms.

Sew 2 rows of machine stitching along each side of cutting sts for front opening. Cut open front opening.

FRONT FACING

With smaller circ needle and RS facing, beg at lower-right edge, and pick up and k20 sts per 4" (10cm) along right front edges, 1 st in from machine stitching, top of sleeves and back neck edges, then down left front to bottom edge; make sure to pick up and k8 (8, 6, 6, 6) sts along top edge of each sleeve.

Working back and forth, beg with a WS row and knit 1 row for fold line.

Work 6 rows of St st, then bind off, making sure to bind off sts along top of fronts, back, and sleeves loosely. Trim cut edges. Fold facing to inside along fold line, covering cut edges, and sew neatly to WS. Mark bottom of front neck shaping on both sides of front.

Mark button placement on left front, placing top button just below beg of front neck shaping, bottom button approx ¾" (2cm) from bottom edge, then evenly space rem buttons in between.

COLLAR

With smaller circ needle and RS facing, beg at bottom of neck shaping on right front, and pick up and k sts through purl ridge to bottom of neck shaping on left front, and place st markers on each side of back, and at center of each sleeve.

Evenly space st markers along each side of front neck edge, dividing sts on each side into 12 sections.

Working back and forth, beg k1, p1 rib and work along left front, top of left sleeve, and across back neck to marker at right back, wrap next st, then turn. Slip first st and tighten it slightly, work rib to marker on left side of back neck, wrap next st, then turn. Slip first st and tighten it slightly, work rib to 2 sts past marker at right back, working wrap and st tog, wrap next st, then turn. Rep this row 3 more times, working 2 more sts at end of each row.

Next row, slip first st and tighten it slightly, work 1 st, (inc 2 sts in next st [working inc sts into rib], work 3 sts) 3 times, work rib to 3 sts before end of back neck, (inc 2 sts in next st [working inc sts into rib], work 3 sts), work 4 more sts, then wrap next st and turn—6 sts increased on each side of neck at shoulders.

Cont working short rows and work to next marker at end of each row, working to last set of sts on each side of front.

It will help to keep track of where the last turn was made by removing each marker as you reach it.

On next RS row, work to last st, then pick up sts along purl ridge to bottom edge. Cut yarn.

With RS facing, pick up and k sts along rem front edge, then work in rib to lower edge on opposite side of front.

Work 3 rows of rib over all sts. Next row, work buttonholes, each over 3 sts where marked on left front edge. Cont rib until button placket measures approx 1¼" (3cm); collar should measure approx 5½" (14cm) along center back. Bind off loosely in rib.

Sew buttons to rib edge at right front, under buttonholes.

CHAPTER 19

Kids' Sweaters

Moss Vest

Sizes
10 (12, 14, 16) years
Sample size is 14 years

Measurements
Chest: 32¹/₂ (34, 35, 36)"/82.5 (86.5, 89, 91.5)cm
Length: 21 (21¹/₂, 22, 22³/₄)"/53.5 (54.5, 56, 58)cm
Armhole: 7 (7¹/₄, 7¹/₂, 7³/₄)"/18 (18.5, 19, 19.5)cm

Yarn
Loop-d-Loop Moss by Teva Durham (85% extra fine merino wool/15% nylon, 163 yd. [147m]/1³/₄ oz. [50g])
3 (3, 4, 5) balls, color #8 Black (MC)
1 (1, 1, 1) ball, color #2 Brown (CC1)
1 (1, 1, 1) ball, color #10 Red (CC2)

Needles and Notions
1 each U.S. size 5 and 6 (3.75mm and 4mm) circular needles, or size needed to obtain gauge
1 set of U.S. size 5 (3.75mm) double-pointed needles—optional
Stitch holders
Stitch markers
Matching sewing thread
Contrasting sewing thread
1 zipper, 7" (18cm)

Gauge
20 sts and 31 rnds over St st using larger needles = 4" (10cm)

➤ Take time to check your gauge.

Warm and comfy, this is the sort of vest a kid can live in. The addition of cutting stitches at the armholes and front opening ensures that you'll be able to work the diamond pattern with ease; you're only stranding two colors at a time while the vertical lines are done using separate strands of yarn for each line, intarsia fashion. Knitting the placket facing in a contrasting colors adds some visual interest as well.

NOTE When working Diamond Pattern, carry MC and CC1 only on rnds 2–4, 6–8, 10–12, 14–16, 18–20, and 22–24; use separate strands of yarn for each CC2 vertical line.

DIRECTIONS

BODY

With smaller circ needle and MC, CO 162 (168, 174, 180) sts. Join and, working in the rnd, make sure sts are not twisted. Mark beg of rnd.

Work 9 rnds of Basket Weave Pattern (page 142).

Change to larger circ needle. Beg St st and inc 0 (2, 0, 2) sts evenly spaced across 1st rnd— 162 (170, 174, 182) sts. Place side markers at the beg of rnd and after 81 (85, 87, 91) sts.

Work even until body measures 13 (13¹/₂, 14, 14¹/₂)"/33 (34.5, 35.5, 37)cm from bottom edge.

PLACKET OPENING

Bind off center 3 sts of front for placket opening, then knit to end of rnd. Next rnd, CO 4 new sts over bound-off sts of previous rnd (these are cutting sts; work in St st throughout and exclude from st counts).

Cont even in St st until body measures 13¹/₂ (13³/₄, 14, 14¹/₂)"/34.5 (35, 35.5, 37)cm from bottom edge, end rnd 4 sts before end of rnd and shape armholes.

ARMHOLES

Bind off the next 8 sts for armhole, knit to 4 sts before next marker, bind off the next 8 sts for armhole then knit to end of rnd—143 (151, 155, 163) sts. CO 4 cutting sts over armhole bound off sts of previous rnd, then cont St st.

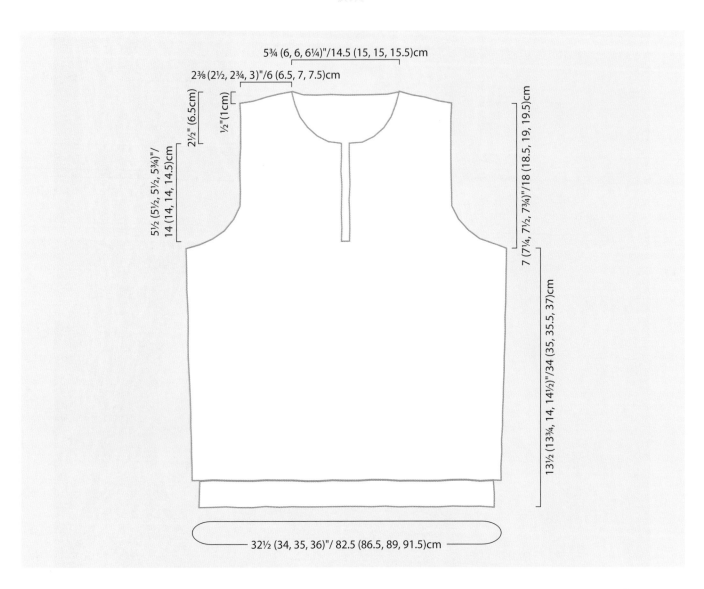

5¾ (6, 6, 6¼)"/14.5 (15, 15, 15.5)cm

2⅜ (2½, 2¾, 3)"/6 (6.5, 7, 7.5)cm

2½" (6.5cm)

½"(1cm)

5½ (5½, 5½, 5¾)"/14 (14, 14, 14.5)cm

7 (7¼, 7½, 7¾)"/18 (18.5, 19, 19.5)cm

13½ (13¾, 14, 14½)"/34 (35, 35.5, 37)cm

32½ (34, 35, 36)"/ 82.5 (86.5, 89, 91.5)cm

Dec 1 st, 1 st in on body at each armhole every other rnd 11 times—99 (107, 111, 119) sts.

At the same time, when body measures 14 (14¼, 15, 15½)"/35.5 (37, 38, 39.5)cm from bottom edge, beg Diamond Pattern, placing center of pattern at center of back, and placing end left front/beg right front on either side of placket cutting sts. When pattern is complete, cont St st with MC and work even until body measures

18½ (19, 19½, 20¼)"/47 (48.5, 49.5, 51.5)cm from bottom edge.

FRONT NECK OPENING

Next rnd, work to 2 (3, 3, 4) sts before placket cutting sts, bind off the next 8 (10, 10, 12) sts for front neck opening (the 4 cutting sts, plus 2 [3, 3, 4] sts on either side), then work to end of rnd—95 (101, 105, 111) sts.

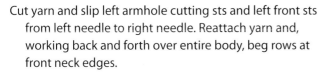

Cut yarn and slip left armhole cutting sts and left front sts from left needle to right needle. Reattach yarn and, working back and forth over entire body, beg rows at front neck edges.

Cont St st and bind off 3 sts at the beg of next 2 rows, 2 sts at the beg of next 4 rows, then dec 1 st at the beg and end of every other row 3 times—75 (81, 85, 91) sts.

BACK NECK OPENING AND SHOULDERS

Next row, work 8 (8, 9, 10) sts, work last 4 (5, 5, 5) sts of front and slip to st holder, bind off armhole cutting sts, work first 4 (5, 5, 5) sts of back and slip to st holder, work 13 (13, 14, 15) sts, bind off the next 17 (19, 19, 21) sts for back neck opening, work 13 (13, 14, 15) sts, work last 4 (5, 5, 5) sts of back and slip to st holder, bind off armhole cutting sts, work first 4 (5, 5, 5) sts of front and slip to st holder, then work rem 8 (8, 9, 10) sts.

FRONT SHOULDERS

Working back and forth over front shoulder, cont St st and at the beg of every other row from armhole edge, slip 4 (4, 5, 5) sts to st holder once. Work 1 more row. Slip all sts back to needle. With RS facing, purl 1 row, then bind off pwise. Complete other side of front to match.

BACK SHOULDERS

Working back shoulders same as front, bind off every other row at neck edge 3 sts once, then 2 sts once.

POCKET

Mark center front st of vest, then 25 (26, 27, 28) sts out on each side of center front st. With larger circ needle, MC and RS facing, pick up and k51 (53, 55, 57) sts between marked sts. Working back and forth, beg with a WS row and work 1 (1½, 1½, 2)"/2.5 (4, 4, 5)cm of St st.

Dec 1 st at the beg and end of every other row 18 (19, 19, 19) times—15 (15, 17, 19) sts.

Work without further dec until pocket measures 5½ (6, 6, 6½)"/14 (15, 15, 16.5)cm. Bind off kwise on WS (or pwise on RS).

POCKET EDGING

With smaller circ needles or dpns, MC and RS facing, pick up and k24 (27, 27, 27) sts along one shaped edge of pocket.

Working back and forth, beg with a WS row and work 5 rows of Basket Weave Pattern.

At the same time, dec 1 st at the beg and end of every other row twice—20 (23, 23, 23) sts. Bind off neatly in pattern and dec 1 st at beg and end of row.

Work edging along rem side of pocket to match.

Pin pocket to front and neatly sew sides and top edges to body.

FINISHING

Block body to finished measurements.

Sew 2 rows of machine stitching, along both sides of cutting sts for armholes and front placket opening. Cut open armholes.

Sew shoulders tog using whip st on RS.

ARMHOLE FACING

With smaller circ needle, MC and with RS facing, beg at bottom of armhole and pick up and k85 (89, 93, 97) sts along one armhole edge. Join and, working in the rnd, mark beg of rnd.

Purl to last 4 sts for fold line, then bind off next 8 sts pwise—77 (81, 85, 89) sts.

Work back and forth, beg with a RS row. Work 5 rows of St st. Bind off kwise on WS. Fold facing to inside along fold line and sew neatly to WS.

ARMHOLE EDGING

With smaller circ needle, MC and with RS facing, beg at bottom of armhole and pick up and k85 (89, 93, 97) sts through purl ridge of fold line and purl sts at bottom of armhole.

Join and, working in the rnd, mark beg of rnd.

Basket Weave Pattern

Diamond Pattern

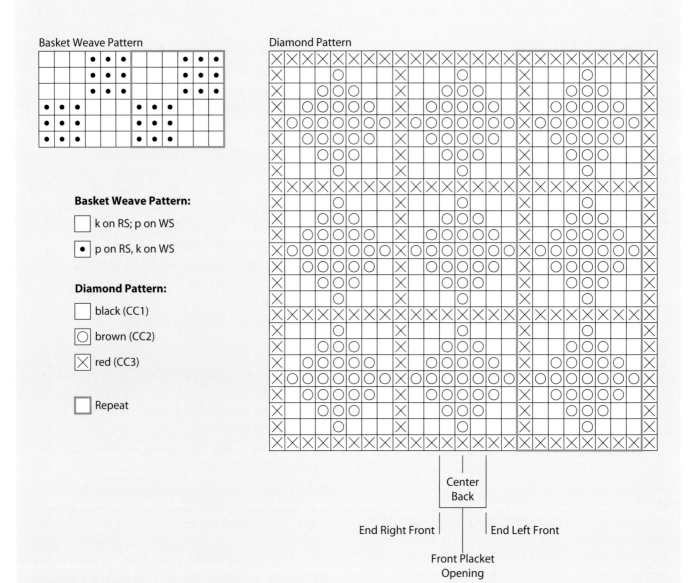

Basket Weave Pattern:

☐ k on RS; p on WS

• p on RS, k on WS

Diamond Pattern:

☐ black (CC1)

Ⓞ brown (CC2)

☒ red (CC3)

☐ Repeat

Center
Back

End Right Front | | End Left Front

Front Placket
Opening

Work 5 rnds of Basket Weave Pattern and dec 1 (5, 3, 1) sts evenly spaced across lower edge of armhole on 1st rnd—84 (84, 90, 96) sts. Bind off neatly in pattern.

Work facing and edging along rem armhole to match.

NECKBAND

Cut open front opening. Fold under each side of opening, along first st in on body side from machine stitching.

With smaller circ needle, MC and with RS facing, beg at right front neck edge and pick up and k71 (77, 77, 83) sts along neck edge, picking up sts through both layers on each side of front opening.

Working back and forth, beg with a WS row. Slip first st of every row, work last st of every row in St st, then work 9 rows of Basket Weave Pattern over rem sts.

Purl 1 row on RS for fold line.

Cont to slip first st of every row and work 2 rows of St st, and dec 1 st at beg and end of second row (dec sts 1 st in from edges).

Work 6 rows of k1, p1 rib. Bind off loosely in rib.

ZIPPER

With smaller circ needle, MC and with RS facing, pick up and k10 sts per 2" (5cm) along one edge of front opening, from bottom of opening to fold line.

Working back and forth, beg with a WS row and bind off neatly pwise.

Work edging along rem side of front opening to match.

Pin zipper into opening, placing top of zipper just below neckband fold line, bottom stop at bottom of opening, and having zipper teeth showing on RS.

Neatly sew zipper to body, working between folded edge of front opening and edging that was just worked.

Fold neckband to inside along fold line and sew loosely to WS, and neatly sew ends of neckband closed, making sure zipper can slide past edges.

With smaller circ needles or dpns and CC2, CO 11 sts.

Working back and forth, work 1" (2.5cm) of St st. Next row, work 3 sts, bind off the next 5 sts, then work rem 3 sts. Working each side of facing separately, cont St st and work even until facing measures 6$\frac{1}{4}$" (16cm). Bind off. Complete other side of facing to match.

Pin facing to back of zipper, with WS tog, and covering cut edges. Neatly sew facing to inside of body along all sides.

Balance Pullover

Sizes
8 (10, 12, 14, 16) years
Sample size is 10 years

Measurements
Chest: 31 (33, 35, 36, 37)"/78.5 (84, 89, 91.5, 94)cm
Body Length: 19 (20½, 21½, 22, 22½)"/48.5 (52, 54.5, 56, 57)cm
Sleeve Length: 14¼ (15¾, 17¼, 18, 18¾)"/36 (40, 44, 45.5, 47.5)cm

Yarn
Balance by O-Wool (50% organic merino wool/50% organic cotton, 130 yd. [120m]/1¾ oz. [50g])
7 (7, 7, 8, 8) skeins, color #3222 Malachite

Needles and Notions
1 U.S. size 6 (4mm) circular needle, or size needed to obtain gauge
1 set U.S. size 6 (4mm) double-pointed needles
Stitch markers
Contrasting sewing thread
1 button, 5/8" (16mm)—JHB International, #83085 Isle of Coco, brown

Gauge
19 sts and 29 rows over Main Pattern, and 21 sts over slip st cables/rib = 4" (10cm)

➤ Take time to check your gauge.

Summer sweaters for kids, especially boys, should be casual and easy to knit. This one fits both of these requirements with the loose-fitting body, and one-button henley-style placket. The neckband is even short-row shaped for rounded corners.

Worked a bit more like a Fair Isle sweater, this one is sewn and cut, then stitches for the sleeves are picked up along the armhole edge and worked to the cuff. Facings are then added to cover up the cut seams.

DIRECTIONS

BODY

With circ needle, CO 148 (156, 164, 168, 176) sts. Join and, working in the rnd, make sure sts are not twisted. Mark beg of rnd and place side marker after 74 (78, 82, 84, 88) sts. Work 1 (1, 1, 1¼, 1¼)"/2.5 (2.5, 2.5, 3, 3)cm of garter rib, beg as shown on chart (page 148).

Beg Main Pattern as shown on chart, and work until body measures 13¼ (13¾, 14¾, 14¼, 14¾)"/33.5 (35, 37.5, 36, 37.5)cm from bottom edge.

Work Arrow Pattern, beg as shown at right-hand side of chart and work 6-st rep 4 (5, 5, 5, 6) times, work center 17 sts, then work 6-st rep on left-hand side of chart to side marker, then beg again at right-hand side of chart and work to end of rnd to make pattern on front and back symmetrical. Knit 1 rnd and inc 12 (16, 16, 20, 16) sts evenly spaced across rnd by lifting horizontal strand between sts and k tbl—160 (172, 180, 188, 192) sts.

PLACKET OPENING

Next row, k1 (1, 3, 0, 0) st(s), beg Yoke pattern as shown on right-hand side of chart and work next 37 (40, 40, 45, 46) sts, bind off the next 4 sts for placket opening, work to 1 (1, 3, 0, 0) st(s) before side marker, k2 (2, 6, 0, 0) sts, beg at right-hand side of chart as before and work 12-st rep to last 1 (1, 3, 0, 0) st(s), end k1 (1, 3, 0, 0) st(s)—156 (168, 176, 184, 188) sts. Cut yarn and slip left front shoulder sts from left needle to right needle. Reattach yarn and, working back and forth, beg rows at front placket opening with a RS row. Cont as est until placket measures 3 (3, 3, 3½, 3½)"/7.5 (7.5, 7.5, 9, 9)cm.

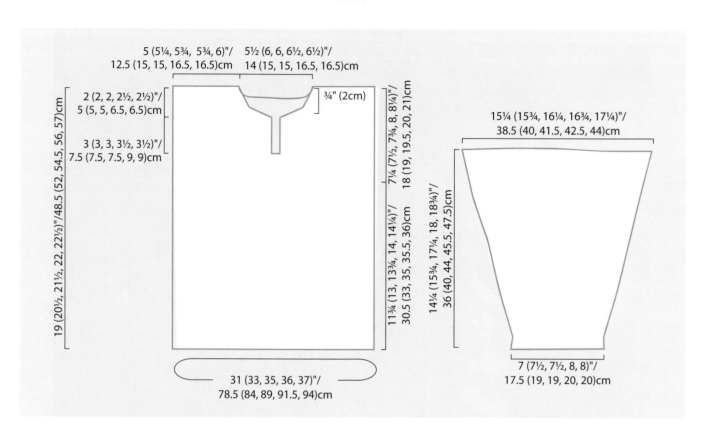

FRONT NECK OPENING

Cont pattern and bind off 3 sts at the beg of next 4 rows, 2 sts at the beg of next 2 (4, 4, 6, 6) rows, then dec 1 st at the beg and end of every other row 3 times. **At the same time,** when body measures 18¼ (19¾, 20¾, 21¼, 21¾)"/46.5 (50, 52.5, 54, 55)cm from bottom edge, shape back neck opening.

BACK NECK OPENING

Cont pattern, rem front neck shaping and work front sts and first 32 (33, 35, 35, 36) sts of back, bind off the next 16 (20, 20, 24, 24) sts for back neck opening, then work to end of row. Working each side of body separately over both front and back of shoulder, cont pattern and

bind off every other row at back neck edge, 3 sts once, then 2 sts once—27 (28, 30, 30, 31) sts. Work even until body measures approx 19 (20¹/₂, 21¹/₂, 22, 22¹/₂)"/48.5 (52, 54.5, 56, 57)cm from bottom edge, ending with a row 1, 6, 7, or 12 of rep. Knit 1 row on WS (or purl 1 row on RS), then bind off. Complete other side of body to match, placing back neck shaping on opposite side.

Place markers at sides of body, 7¹/₄ (7¹/₂, 7³/₄, 8, 8¹/₄)"/18.5 (19, 19.5, 20.5, 21)cm down from purl row at top of shoulders for bottom of armholes. Sew 2 rows of machine stitching, 2 sts out from where side markers were placed and across the bottom of the 4 sts for armholes. Cut open armholes. Sew shoulders tog using whip st through purl rows at top of shoulders.

SLEEVES

With larger circ needle and RS facing, beg at bottom of armhole and pick up and k72 (74, 76, 78, 82) sts along armhole edge. Join and, working in the rnd, mark beg of rnd and beg rnds at center of underarm.

Beg Main Pattern, placing center of chart at center of sleeve and count back on chart to locate beg point of pattern. **At the same time,** dec 1 st at the beg and end of every 4th rnd 4 (0, 0, 0, 0) times, every 5th rnd 15 (11, 10, 5, 11) times, then every 6th rnd 0 (8, 10, 15, 11) times, leaving 2 sts between dec sts—34 (36, 36, 38, 38) sts.

Work even until sleeve measures 13$\frac{1}{4}$ (14$\frac{3}{4}$, 16$\frac{1}{4}$, 16$\frac{3}{4}$, 17$\frac{1}{2}$)"/33.5 (37.5, 41.5, 42.5, 44.5)cm, ending with an even number rnd of rep. Work 1 (1, 1, 1$\frac{1}{4}$, 1$\frac{1}{4}$)"/2.5 (2.5, 2.5, 3, 3)cm of garter rib, ending with an even number rnd of rep. Bind off loosely kwise.

Make second sleeve to match.

FINISHING

Block pieces to finished measurements.

SLEEVE FACINGS

Turn sweater with WS facing. With circ needle and RS of cut edge facing, beg at bottom of armhole and pick up and k78 (80, 82, 84, 86) sts along armhole, making sure to pick up sts through same rows and sts where sleeve sts were picked up. Join and, working in the rnd, mark beg of rnd and beg rnds at bottom of armhole. Work St st so that purl side will be next to WS of body when sewn over cut edge. Work 5 rnds of St st and, **at the same time,** inc 1 st at the beg and end of 1st, 3rd, and 5th rnds, leaving 2 sts between inc sts. Bind off loosely. Turn facing toward body, covering cut edge, then loosely sew to WS. Work edging along rem armhole to match.

BUTTON PLACKET

With dpns or circ needle and RS facing, pick up and k15 (15, 15, 17, 17) sts along right edge of placket opening. Working back and forth, beg with a WS row and knit 3 rows. Work 5 rows of St st. Bind off kwise on WS.

BUTTONHOLE PLACKET

Pick up sts along left front edge of opening in same manner as button placket. Working back and forth, beg with a WS row and knit 4 rows.

Next row (WS), k12 (12, 12, 14, 14) sts, yo, k2tog for buttonhole, end k1. Knit 3 rows. Bind off kwise.

NECKBAND

With circ needle and RS facing, pick up and k9 sts per 2" (5cm) along neck edge and ends of plackets. Working back and forth, beg with a WS row. Knit 3 rows.

Next row, knit to 2 sts before end of row, slip next st pwise, wrap next st, then turn.

Next row, slip next st and tighten it slightly, knit to 2 sts before end of row, wrap next st, then turn. Rep this row once more, working to 4 sts before end of row before wrapping and turning. Rep this row once more, working to end of row. Bind off all sts kwise. Sew button to right placket under buttonhole.

Arrow Pattern

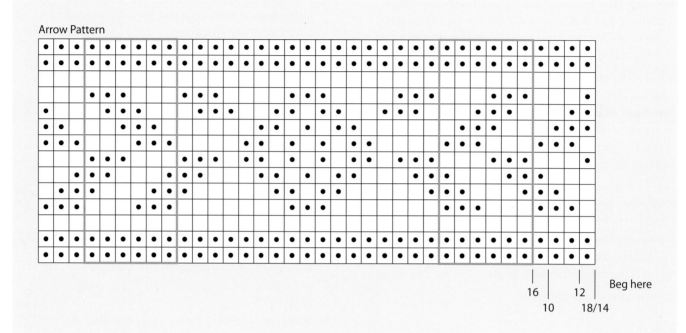

16   12   Beg here
10   18/14

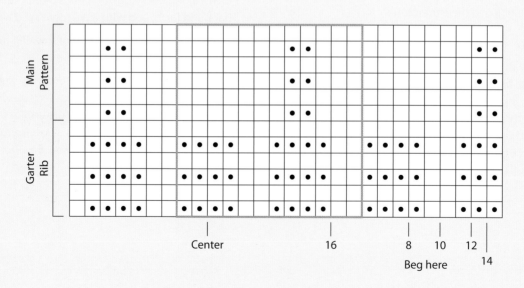

Center   16   8   10   12

Beg here   14

Yoke Pattern

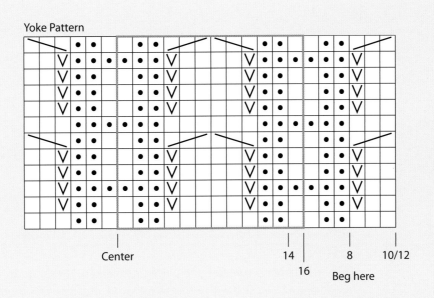

Center   14   8   10/12

16

Beg here

Sleeve Pattern

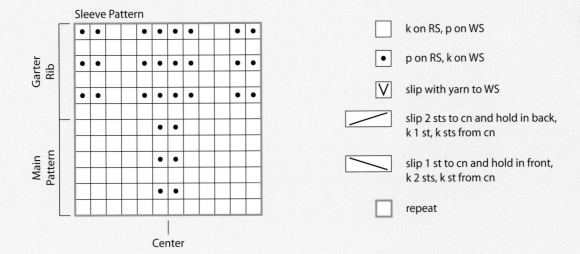

	k on RS, p on WS
•	p on RS, k on WS
V	slip with yarn to WS
╱	slip 2 sts to cn and hold in back, k 1 st, k sts from cn
╲	slip 1 st to cn and hold in front, k 2 sts, k st from cn
▢	repeat

Garter Rib

Main Pattern

Center

Sizes

8 (10, 12, 14, 16) years
Sample size is 16 years

Measurements

Chest: 32 (34, 36, 37, 38)"/81.5 (86.5, 91.5, 94, 96.5)cm
Length: 18 (19, 20, 20½, 21)"/45.5 (48.5, 51, 52, 53.5)cm
Sleeve Length to Underarm: 14 (15½, 17, 17¾, 18½)"/35.5 (39.5, 43, 45, 47)cm

Yarn

Daylily by Nashua Handknits (46% cotton/ 31% acrylic/23% nylon, 87 yd. [80m]/ 1¾ oz. [50g] ball)
10 (11, 11, 12, 13) balls, color #8739 Purple

Needles and Notions

1 U.S. size 7 (4.5mm) circular needle
1 U.S. size 8 (5mm) circular needle, or size needed to obtain gauge
1 set each U.S. sizes 7 and 8 (4.5mm and 5mm) double-pointed needles
Stitch holders
Stitch markers
Contrasting sewing thread
Matching sewing thread, pins, and sewing needle
7 (8, 8, 8, 8) buttons, ¾" (20mm)—Moving Mud glass buttons
1¼ (1¼, 1¼, 1½, 1½) yd./114 (114, 114, 137, 137)cm ribbon (¾" (2cm) wide to 1½" (4cm) wide—Wright's ¾" (20mm) wide multi woven braid, #7835002

NOTE If using a narrow (less than ¾" [2cm] wide) ribbon and a wider band is desired, purchase about ¼ yd. (23cm) more than twice the amount of ribbon listed above, and sew the two bands together along one edge when finishing the cardigan. The extra ribbon will be needed at the lower edges of the armhole.

Gauge

16 sts and 23 rows over St st using larger needles = 4" (10cm)

➤ Take time to check gauge.

Daylily Hooded Cardigan

Even simple cardigans can be knit using the Norwegian construction methods, as this design illustrates. It's also a chance to add a little glam to a plain garment by introducing a fun patterned ribbon. Using the ribbon at the armholes also helps to reduce the bulk around the armhole when using a medium weight yarn such as the one used here.

DIRECTIONS

BODY

With smaller circ needle, CO 126 (134, 142, 146, 150) sts. Working back and forth, knit 4 rows.

Change to larger circ needle and place side markers 31 (33, 35, 36, 37) sts from beg and end of row. Beg St st with a RS row and work until body measures 11½ (12¼, 12¾, 13, 13)"/29 (31, 32.5, 33, 33)cm from bottom edge.

ARMHOLES

Next row, work first 24 (26, 28, 29, 30) sts, bind off the next 14 sts for armhole, work next 50 (54, 58, 60, 62) sts, bind off the next 14 sts for armhole, then work to end of row—98 (106, 114, 118, 122) sts. Next row, CO 4 new sts over each armhole (these are cutting sts; work in reverse St st throughout and exclude from st counts).

Work even until body measures 15¾ (16¾, 17½, 18, 18½)"/40 (42.5, 44.5, 45.5, 47)cm from bottom edge.

FRONT NECK OPENING

Bind off 3 sts at the beg of next 4 rows, 2 sts at the beg of next 2 rows, then dec 1 st at the beg and end of every other row 1 (1, 2, 2, 3) times. **At the same time,** when body measures 17½ (18½, 19½, 20, 20½)"/44.5 (47, 49.5, 51, 52)cm from bottom edge, shape back neck opening.

BACK NECK OPENING

Work front sts and cont any rem neck shaping, work first 18 (20, 21, 22, 22) sts of back, join another ball of yarn, bind off the next 14 (14, 16, 16, 18) sts for neck opening, then work to end of row. Working each side of body separately over front and back of same shoulder, bind off at back neck edge every other row 2 sts once, then 1 st once—30 (34, 36, 38, 38) sts rem on each side of body (15 [17, 18, 19, 19] for front

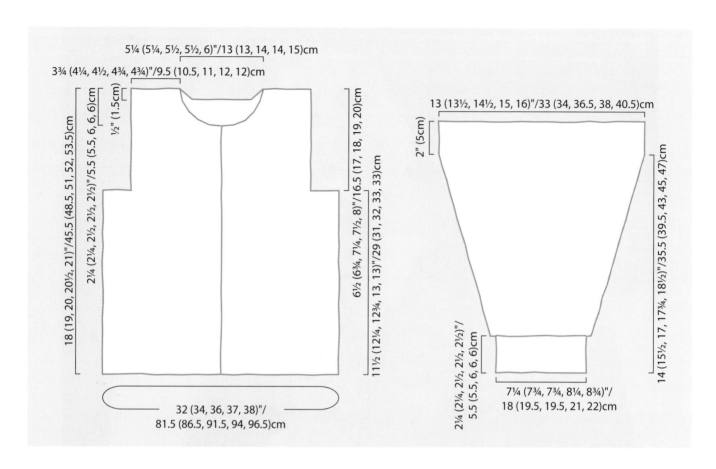

5¼ (5¼, 5½, 5½, 6)"/13 (13, 14, 14, 15)cm

3¾ (4¼, 4½, 4¾, 4¾)"/9.5 (10.5, 11, 12, 12)cm

½" (1.5cm)

18 (19, 20, 20½, 21)"/45.5 (48.5, 51, 52, 53.5)cm

2¼ (2¼, 2½, 2½, 2½)"/5.5 (5.5, 6, 6, 6)cm

6½ (6¾, 7¼, 7½, 8)"/16.5 (17, 18, 19, 20)cm

11½ (12¼, 12¾, 13, 13)"/29 (31, 32, 33, 33)cm

32 (34, 36, 37, 38)"/
81.5 (86.5, 91.5, 94, 96.5)cm

13 (13½, 14½, 15, 16)"/33 (34, 36.5, 38, 40.5)cm

2" (5cm)

14 (15½, 17, 17, 17¾, 18½)"/35.5 (39.5, 43, 45, 47)cm

2¼ (2¼, 2½, 2½, 2½)"/5.5 (5.5, 6, 6, 6)cm

7¼ (7¾, 7¾, 8¼, 8¾)"/
18 (19.5, 19.5, 21, 22)cm

and back of each shoulder, plus cutting sts). Body should measure approx 18 (19, 20, 20½, 21)"/45.5 (48.5, 51, 52, 53.5)cm from bottom edge. Bind off the 4 cutting sts over each armhole on last row. Slip rem 15 (17, 18, 19, 19) sts on both front and back shoulders to st holders. Complete other side of body to match.

BUTTON PLACKET

With smaller circ needle and RS facing, beg at neck edge and pick up and k63 (67, 70, 72, 74) sts along left front opening to bottom edge.

Working back and forth, beg with a WS row and work approx 1" (2.5cm) of garter st, ending with a RS row. Bind off neatly kwise on WS.

Mark placement for buttons along placket, placing top button ½" (1.5cm) from neck edge and bottom button ½" (1.5cm) from bottom edge, and evenly spacing rem buttons in between.

BUTTONHOLE PLACKET

With smaller circ needle and RS facing, beg at bottom edge and pick up and k63 (67, 70, 72, 74) sts along right front opening to neck edge.

Working back and forth, beg with a WS and knit 2 rows.

Next row, work buttonholes, each over 2 sts as marked on button placket, making buttonholes by binding off 2 sts for each, then on next row CO 2 new sts over bound-off sts of previous row.

Cont garter st until placket measures approx 1" (2.5cm), ending with a RS row. Bind off neatly kwise on WS.

SLEEVES

With smaller dpns, CO 24 (26, 26, 28, 30) sts. Join and, working in the rnd, make sure sts are not twisted. Mark beg of rnd. Work $2^1/_4$ ($2^1/_4$, $2^1/_2$, $2^1/_2$, $2^1/_2$)"/5.5 (5.5, 6.5, 6.5, 6.5)cm of k1, p1 rib.

Change to larger dpns. Knit 1 rnd and inc 5 sts evenly spaced across rnd—29 (31, 31, 33, 35) sts.

Cont St st and, **at the same time,** inc 1 st at the beg and end of every 6th rnd 2 (12, 10, 14, 12) times, then every 5th rnd 10 (0, 4, 0, 3) times, leaving 2 sts between inc sts—53 (55, 59, 61, 65) sts.

Work even until sleeve measures 14 ($15^1/_2$, 17, $17^3/_4$, $18^1/_2$)"/35.5 (39.5, 43, 45, 47)cm from bottom of rib.

Sleeve Cap

Working back and forth, cont St st and work until sleeve cap measures 2" (5cm). Slip sts to st holder.

Make second sleeve to match.

HOOD

With smaller circ needle, CO 96 (100, 104, 108, 112) sts. Working back and forth, knit 4 rows.

Change to larger circ needle and place center marker after 48 (50, 52, 54, 56) sts. Beg St st with a RS row and work until hood measures $3/_4$ ($3/_4$, 1, 1, $1^1/_4$)"/2 (2, 2.5, 2.5, 3)cm from bottom edge. Dec 1 st, 1 st in from edges, at the beg and end of every other row 10 times—76 (80, 84, 88, 92) sts.

Work even until hood measures $5^1/_2$ ($5^1/_2$, $5^3/_4$, $5^3/_4$, 6)"/14 (14, 14.5, 14.5, 15)cm from bottom edge, ending with a WS row.

SHAPING

Dec 1 st on each side of center marker every RS row 8 times, leaving 4 sts between dec sts—60 (64, 68, 72, 76) sts.

Work 1 row even. Divide sts evenly on 2 needles and hold with RS tog. Using a third needle, work three-needle bind-off method to join hood to center of top.

FINISHING

Block pieces to finished measurements.

Sew 2 rows of machine stitching along each side of cutting sts at armholes. For this cardigan, it will be easier to do the machine sewing from the WS. Cut open armholes.

With WS held tog, slip sts for front and back of one shoulder to circ needle, alternating 1 st from front, then 1 st from back. *Pass second st on left needle over first st and off needle, knit first st—1 st on right needle. Rep from * once more—2 sts on left needle. Pass first st on right needle over second st to bind-off—1 st rem on right needle. Rep from * to end of row. Fasten off. Rep with rem shoulder.

With WS of body and sleeves facing, and with cut edge to outside, sew sleeves to armhole using Kitchener st to sew live sts from sleeves to vertical edges of armholes, working in space between cutting sts and side of body. Neatly sew open edges of sleeve caps to bound off sts at bottom of armholes.

Cut 2 pieces of ribbon the length of armhole plus 1" (2.5cm) to miter at lower corners of armholes plus 1" (2.5cm) for seam allowances. Pin ribbon to body, covering cut edges, and miter at lower corners of armhole, having ends of ribbon meet at center under sleeve. Fold under approx $1/_2$" (1.5cm) at each end. With matching sewing thread, neatly sew ribbon to body and sleeves, making sure to sew fold at mitered corners to ribbon, and folded ends tog at underarm.

NECKBAND

With smaller circ needle and RS facing, pick up and k63 (63, 66, 66, 69) sts along neck edge and ends of plackets. Working back and forth, beg with a WS row and knit 2 rows. Bind off loosely kwise on WS.

Pin shaped edge of hood into neck opening along WS of neckband. Neatly sew hood to neck edge.

Sew buttons to left placket as marked. If desired, sew around buttonholes with buttonhole stitch to reinforce the edges of the holes.

Terra Tunic

Sizes
10 (12, 14, 16) years
Sample size is 16 years

Measurements
Bust: 30 (32, 33, 34)"/76 (81.5, 84, 86.5)cm
Body Length: 25 (26, 27, 28)"/63.5 (66, 68.5, 71)cm
Sleeve Length: 13½ (14½, 15, 15½)"/34.5 (37, 38, 39.5)cm

Yarn
Terra by South West Trading Company (50% bamboo/50% cotton, 120 yd. [110m]/1¾ oz. [50g])
8 (9, 9, 10) balls, color #436 Rose Quartz

Needles and Notions
1 each U.S. size 4 and 6 (3.5mm and 4mm) circular needles, or size needed to obtain gauge
1 set each U.S. size 4 and 6 (3.5mm and 4mm) double-pointed needles, or size needed to obtain gauge
Crochet hook U.S. size D/3 (3mm)
Stitch holders
Stitch markers
Contrasting sewing thread

Gauge
22 sts and 17 rnds over lace pattern using larger needles = 4" (10cm) (unstretched)
22 sts and 28 rnds over St st using smaller needles = 4" (10cm)

➤ Take time to check your gauge.

I love the soft drape of this bamboo/cotton blend yarn. The lace pattern in the skirt is based on a classic Shetland lace pattern, just worked on a larger needle.

Because the longer body adds weight to the piece as you work, this pattern is a great example of when it's a good idea to add cutting stitches and continue the front and back in one piece after reaching the armholes. One might think that cutting into a garment knit with such a soft yarn might result in a tangled mesh. This tunic turned out so well I've been thinking of making one in a larger size for myself.

DIRECTIONS
KNITTED PLEATS
Left Facing Pleat

Slip next 8 (8, 9, 9) sts to dpn for face of pleat, slip next 8 (8, 9, 9) sts to second dpn for fold-under. Turn dpns so that WS of face and fold-under are tog, then turn so that RS of fold-under and underlay (next sts of body) are tog, with dpns to RS of work. *Knit tog 1 st from both dpns and next body st (1 st made from 3); rep from * until all sts have been worked from dpns.

Right Facing Pleat

Slip next 16 (16, 18, 18) sts to dpns same as for left facing pleat; sts on first dpn are the underlay, sts on second dpn are the fold-under, and next 8 (8, 9, 9) sts on main needle are the face. Turn dpns so that WS of face and fold-under are tog, then turn again so that RS of fold-under and underlay are tog, with dpns to WS of work. Work sts tog same as for left facing pleat.

SKIRT

With larger circ needle, CO 224 (238, 252, 266) sts. Working back and forth, knit 1 row but do not turn. Join and, working in the rnd, make sure sts are not twisted. Mark beg of rnd. Purl 1 rnd. Work 1 eyelet rnd (*yo, k2tog; rep from * to end of rnd), then knit 1 rnd.

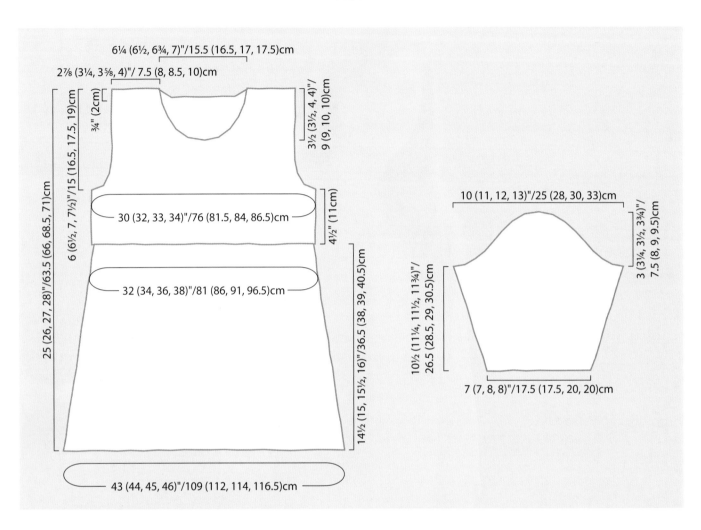

6¼ (6½, 6¾, 7)"/15.5 (16.5, 17, 17.5)cm

2⅞ (3¼, 3⅝, 4)"/ 7.5 (8, 8.5, 10)cm

¾" (2cm)

3½ (3½, 4, 4)"/ 9 (9, 10, 10)cm

15 (16.5, 17.5, 19)cm

6 (6½, 7, 7½)"/

30 (32, 33, 34)"/76 (81.5, 84, 86.5)cm

4½" (11cm)

25 (26, 27, 28)"/63.5 (66, 68.5, 71)cm

32 (34, 36, 38)"/81 (86, 91, 96.5)cm

14½ (15, 15½, 16)"/36.5 (38, 39, 40.5)cm

43 (44, 45, 46)"/109 (112, 114, 116.5)cm

10 (11, 12, 13)"/25 (28, 30, 33)cm

3 (3¼, 3½, 3¾)"/ 7.5 (8, 9, 9.5)cm

10½ (11¼, 11½, 11¾)"/ 26.5 (28.5, 29, 30.5)cm

7 (7, 8, 8)"/17.5 (17.5, 20, 20)cm

Beg Lace Pattern and work until skirt measures 14¹/₂ (15, 15¹/₂, 16)"/37 (38, 39.5, 40.5)cm from lowest point at bottom edge, ending with a rnd 1 of rep.

Pleats

Next rnd, k22 (24, 23, 25) sts, *work left facing pleat as directed above, k next 20 (23, 26, 29) sts, work right facing pleat, k44 (48, 46, 50) sts; rep from * once more, ending rep k22 (24, 23, 25) sts—160 (174, 180, 194) sts.

Change to smaller circ needle and place side markers at the beg of rnd and after 80 (87, 90, 96) sts. Knit 1 rnd and

dec 0 (0, 0, 4) sts evenly spaced across rnd—160 (174, 180, 190) sts. Purl 1 rnd, knit 1 rnd, then purl 1 rnd.

BODICE

Beg St st and work even until body measures 4¹/₂" (11.5cm) above pleats, ending last rnd 3 sts before end of rnd.

Bind off the next 6 sts for armhole, knit next 74 (81, 84, 89) sts, bind off the next 6 sts for armhole, then knit to end of rnd—148 (162, 168, 178) sts. CO 4 new sts over bound-off sts of previous rnd at both armholes (these are cutting sts; work in St st and exclude from st counts),

then join and cont working in the rnd; beg rnds at center of cutting sts at left side of bodice. **At the same time,** dec 1 st before and after cutting sts at both armholes every other rnd 3 (4, 3, 3) times—136 (146, 156, 166) sts.

Work even until bodice measures 7 (7$\frac{1}{2}$, 7$\frac{1}{2}$, 8)"/18 (19, 19, 20.5)cm from top of pleats.

FRONT NECK OPENING

Next rnd, knit the first 32 (34, 36, 38) sts (the 2 cutting sts, plus next 30 [32, 34, 36] sts), bind off the next 8 (9, 10, 11) sts for front neck opening, then knit to end of rnd—128 (137, 146, 155) sts. Cut yarn and slip left front shoulder sts from left needle to right needle. Reattach yarn and, working back and forth, beg rows at front neck edges.

Cont St st and bind off 3 sts at the beg of first 2 rows, then 2 sts at the beg of next 6 rows. Dec 1 st at the beg and end of every RS row twice, then every other RS row twice—102 (111, 120, 129) sts.

Work without further shaping until bodice measures approx 9$\frac{3}{4}$ (10$\frac{1}{4}$, 10$\frac{3}{4}$, 11$\frac{1}{4}$)"/25 (26, 27.5, 28.5)cm from top of pleats.

BACK NECK OPENING

Next row, work front, cutting sts and first 23 (25, 27, 29) sts of back, bind off the next 22 (23, 24, 25) sts for back neck opening, then work to end of row.

Working each side of body separately, working over both front and back, cont St st and bind off every other row at back neck edge, 3 sts twice—34 (38, 42, 46) sts.

Work even until bodice measures 10$\frac{1}{2}$ (11, 11$\frac{1}{2}$, 12)"/26.5 (28, 29, 30.5)cm from top of pleats, and bind off the 4 cutting sts at each armhole. Slip rem sts to holders. Complete other side of body to match, placing back neck shaping on opposite side.

SLEEVES

With larger dpns, CO 42 sts. Working back and forth, knit 1 row but do not turn. Join and, working in the rnd, make sure sts are not twisted. Mark beg of rnd. Purl 1 rnd. Work 1 eyelet rnd (*yo, k2tog; rep from * to end of rnd), then knit 1 rnd. Work 3 rnds of Lace pattern.

Change to smaller dpns. Knit 1 rnd and dec 4 (4, 0, 0) sts evenly spaced across rnd—38 (38, 42, 42) sts. Beg St st and, **at the same time,** inc 1 st at the beg and end of every 6th rnd 9 (11, 6, 0) times, every 5th rnd 0 (0, 6, 8) times, then every 4th rnd 0 (0, 0, 7) times, leaving 2 sts between inc sts—56 (60, 66, 72) sts.

Work even until sleeve measures 10$\frac{1}{2}$ (11$\frac{1}{4}$, 11$\frac{1}{2}$, 11$\frac{3}{4}$)"/26.5 (28.5, 29, 30)cm from lowest point at bottom edge, ending last rnd 3 sts before end of rnd.

Sleeve Cap

Bind off the next 6 sts for underarm, then knit to end of rnd—50 (54, 60, 66) sts. Working back and forth, cont St st and bind off 3 sts at the beg of first 2 rows, then 2 sts at the beg of next 4 rows. Dec 1 st at the beg and end of every other row 6 (5, 5, 6) times. Bind off 2 sts at the beg of next 2 (4, 6, 6) rows, then 3 sts at the beg of next 2 rows. Bind off rem 14 (16, 18, 22) sts.

Make second sleeve to match.

$\square$ = k

$\boxed{O}$ = yo

$\boxed{/}$ = k4tog (or k2tog, slip st back to left needle
        pass next 2 sts over, then slip st back to right needle)

$\boxed{\backslash}$ = k4tog tbl (or slip 2 sts kwise, k2tog tbl, then psso)

$\square$ = repeat

Finishing

Block pieces to finished measurements.

Sew 2 rows of machine stitching along both sides of cutting sts at armholes. Cut open armholes.

Slip sts for front and back of same shoulder to smaller needles. Holding needles as if to knit, *insert right needle into back of first 2 sts on left needle and k tog, slip st back to left needle. Insert left needle into front of first 2 sts on right needle and k tog, slip st back to right needle. Rep from * until 1 st rem on both needles. Slip st on right needle to left needle, then lift second st over first and off needle. Fasten off rem st. Rep with rem shoulder.

Neckband

With smaller circ needle and RS facing, beg at left shoulder and pick up and k11 sts per 2" (5cm) along neck edge (total number of sts picked up should be divisible by 4). Join and, working in the rnd, mark beg of rnd. (Purl 1 rnd, knit 1 rnd) twice. Next rnd, *k2, k2tog, yo; rep from * to end of rnd. Knit 1 rnd. Bind off pwise.

Armhole Seams And Facings

Pin sleeves into armholes, with centers of sleeves at shoulder seams. Neatly sew sleeves to body, sewing into body on first st away from machine stitching toward body.

On inside, with smaller circ needle and RS of facing forward, pick up and k11 sts per 2" (5cm) along cut edge only of armhole seam, picking sts up along line of where sleeve was sewn into armhole. Working back and forth, work 4 rows of St st. Bind off kwise on WS. Turn facing toward body, covering cut edges, then neatly sew facing to WS.

CHAPTER 20

Accessories

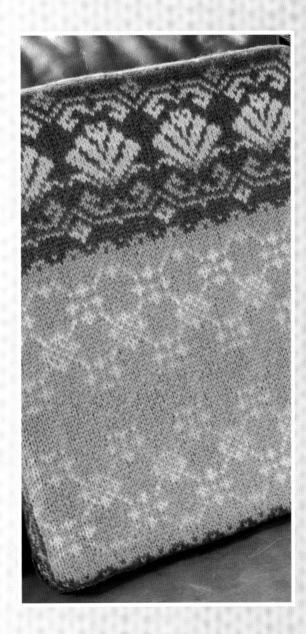

Blue Sky Wrap

Everyone loves a soft, warm blanket but it's not practical to drag one along with you after a certain age. This wrap is the next best thing. Worked as a large rectangle, the sleeves are attached to vertical slits at the sides, with the patterned facings sewn to the right side.

The sleeves of this wrap are extra long; wear them either folded into a cuff or leave them long so they extend down over part of your hand. Secure the front below the collar with a dramatic shawl pin. Any way you wear it, this is one piece that's sure to get compliments.

DIRECTIONS

BODY

With smaller circ needle and MC, CO 211 (243, 263, 287) sts. Working back and forth, work 1¼" (3cm) of St st, ending with a RS row and CO 5 new sts at end of row. Knit 1 row for fold line and CO 5 new sts at end of row—221 (253, 273, 297) sts.

Change to larger circ needle. Next row, slip 1 st, (k1, p1) twice, purl to last 5 sts, (p1, k1) twice, k1. Next row, slip 1 st, (p1, k1) twice, knit to last 5 sts, (k1, p1) twice, p1. Rep last 2 rows. Maintaining first 5 sts and last 5 sts as est throughout, work 12 rows of Main Pattern (page 163) on center sts. Cont in St st and work Pattern A, then purl 1 row for fold line with MC on center sts.

Cont Main Pattern on center sts until body measures 24½" (62cm) from fold line, ending with a row 3 or 7 of rep.

ARMHOLES

Next row, work first 63 (78, 86, 98) sts, bind off 3 sts for bottom of armhole, work next 89 (91, 95, 95) sts, bind off 3 sts for bottom of armhole, then work to end of row.

CO 3 new sts over bound-off sts of previous row, then cont working until body measures approx 33 (33½, 34, 34½)"/84 (85, 86.5, 87.5)cm from fold line, working new CO sts in k1, p1, k1 rib.

Next row, work first 63 (78, 86, 98) sts, bind off 3 sts for top of armhole, work next 89 (91, 95, 95) sts, bind off 3 sts for top of armhole, then work to end of row.

Sizes
XS/S (M/L, XL, XXL)
Sample size is XS/S

Measurements
Bust: 42 (48, 52, 56)"/106.5 (122, 132, 142) cm
Body Length: 45 (45½, 46, 47)"/114.5 (115.5, 117, 119.5)cm
Sleeve Length: 23½ (24, 24½, 25)"/59.5 (61, 62, 63.5)cm

Yarn
Blue Sky Sport Weight by Blue Sky Alpacas (100% baby alpaca, 110 yd. [100m]/1¾ oz. [50g])
18 (21, 23, 24) skeins, color #502 Natural Copper (MC)
2 (2, 2, 3) skeins, color #541 Molasses (CC1)
2 (2, 3, 3) skeins, color #522 Denim (CC2)
1 (1, 2, 2) skein(s), color #542 Currant (CC3)

Needles and Notions
1 each U.S. size 5 and 6 (3.75mm and 4mm) circular needles, or size needed to obtain gauge
1 set each U.S. size 5 and 6 (3.75mm and 4mm) double-pointed needles, or size needed to obtain gauge
Stitch markers
Cable needle—optional
Blunt tapestry needle
Contrasting sewing thread
Square Shawl Pin by Annie Adams Adornment

Gauge
21 sts and 29 rows over Main Pattern using larger needles = 4" (10cm)
22 sts and 26 rnds over color work using larger needles = 4" (10cm)

➤ Take time to check your gauge.

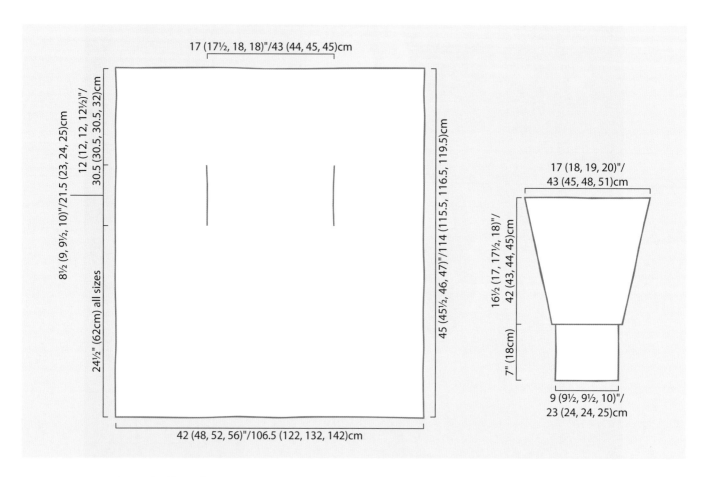

CO 3 new sts over bound-off sts of previous row, then work 1¹/₂" (4cm) of Main Pattern, ending with a row 4 or 8 of rep. Work 3" (7.5cm) of k1, p1 rib, following rib as est at front edges, and ending with a WS row.

COLLAR

Purl 1 row. WS of work now becomes RS.

Work 2 (2, 2, 2¹/₂)"/5 (5, 5, 6.5)cm of Main Pattern, ending with a row 4 or 8 of rep.

Beg St st and work Pattern A. Purl 1 row with MC.

Work 12 rows of Main Pattern.

Knit 1 row, then work 3 rows of reverse St st and bind off first 5 sts on last 2 rows—211 (243, 263, 287) sts.

Change to smaller circ needle and work 1¹/₄" (3cm) of St st. Bind off loosely.

SLEEVES

With smaller dpns and MC, CO 48 (52, 52, 56) sts. Join and, working in the rnd, make sure sts are not twisted. Mark beg of rnd.

Work 7" (18cm) of k2, p2 rib and inc 9 sts evenly spaced across last rnd—57 (61, 61, 65) sts.

Change to larger dpns. Beg Pattern B (page 164), placing center st of chart at center of sleeve. **At the same time,** inc 1 st at the beg and end of every 5th rnd 21 (18, 12, 12) times, then every 4th rnd 0 (4, 12, 13) times, leaving 2 sts between inc sts and working inc sts into pattern—99 (105, 109, 115) sts.

Main Pattern

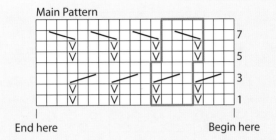

End here   Begin here

Pattern A

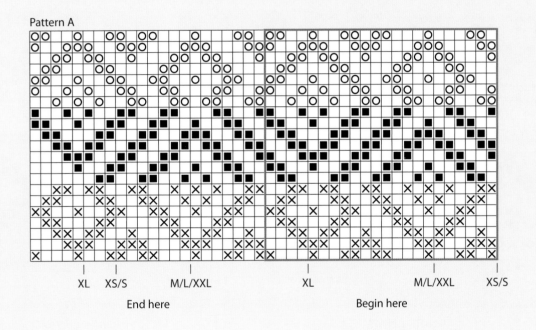

XL   XS/S   M/L/XXL   XL   M/L/XXL   XS/S

End here   Begin here

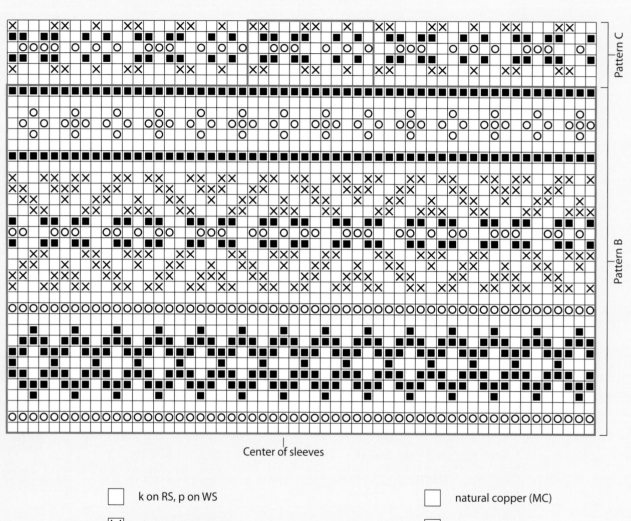

Center of sleeves

	k on RS, p on WS		natural copper (MC)
	slip with yarn to WS		mollasses (CC1)
	slip 2 sts to cn and hold in back, k 1 st, k sts from cn		denim (CC2)
	slip 1 st to cn and hold in front, k 2 sts, k st from cn		currant (CC3)
			repeat

Work even until sleeve measures 23¹/₂ (24, 24¹/₂, 25)"/59.5 (61, 62, 63.5)cm from bottom of rib, and ending with a solid color rnd if possible.

Purl 1 rnd with last color used.

Facing

Work Pattern C and, **at the same time**, inc 1 st at the beg and end of 1st rnd, then every other rnd in same manner as sleeve underarm inc—105 (111, 115, 121) sts.

Cut yarn, leaving an end long enough to sew around armhole (approx 3 times the distance around outer edge of sleeve facing). Slip sts to scrap yarn and set sleeve aside.

Make second sleeve to match.

FINISHING

Block pieces to finished measurements. Fold lower edge of body and edge of collar to inside along 3 rows of reverse St st and sew neatly to WS, allowing reverse St st to show along edges.

Sew 2 rows of machine stitching along each side of cutting sts for armholes. Cut between machine seams.

Pin sleeves into armholes, with RS tog and center of sleeve at top of armhole. Turn work with WS of body facing and sleeve facing extending to RS. Using whip st, sew through 1 st of body, 1 st in from machine seams, and both loops of last 2 rows of sleeve before the facing.

On RS, slip live sts from top edge of sleeve facing to dpns as you work, and pin facing to body. Using long tail from top of facing and back st, sew facing to outside of body, covering cut edges. To work back st, insert needle into fabric at first st, bring needle up to RS in second st, back down into first st, up at third st, down into second st, up at fourth st, down into third st. Cont as est to last st, then work final st by coming up at first st, then back down into last st. Fasten securely.

Soft Linen Box Pillow

Size
16" × 16" (40.5cm × 40.5cm)

Yarn
Soft Linen by Classic Elite Yarns (30% alpaca/35% wool/35% linen, 137 yd. [126m]/1³/₄ oz. [50g])
3 balls, color #2248 Blue Grotto (MC)
2 balls, color #2251 Loden Green (CC1)
1 ball, color #2225 Smoky Rose (CC2)
1 ball, color #2250 Inca Gold (CC3)
1 ball, color #2275 Linen (CC4)

Needles and Notions
2 each U.S. size 5 (3.75mm) circular needles—32" (80cm) long, or size to obtain gauge
Stitch markers
Contrasting sewing thread
Matching sewing thread
Zipper 20" (51cm)
Box pillow form 16" (40.5cm), or 16" (40.5cm) square piece of foam, approx 2" (5cm) thick

Gauge
24 sts and 28 rnds over color work pattern = 4" (10cm)

➤ Take the time to check your gauge.

Pillows are a good way to try out new techniques. Small enough to make fairly quickly, they also make a nice break from larger projects, yield a finished piece more quickly than adult-size sweaters, and don't usually involve complex construction.

While this particular design may be a bit more involved than your average pillow, the only sewing done on this pillow is the machine stitching to cut apart the front and back, and sewing in the zipper. The rest of the assembly is done by picking up stitches and using three-needle bind off. Pretty good payoff for a stand-out design inspired by jacquard fabric patterns.

DIRECTIONS

PILLOW
With CC1, CO 192 sts. Join and, working in the rnd, make sure sts are not twisted. Mark beg of rnd.

Set up pattern in this manner: Work 3 side sts, place marker, beg as shown on chart (page 168), then work 16-st rep of Main Pattern over next 80 sts, work next 6 sts, place marker, work side sts over next 5 sts (the last 2 sts at left side of chart, then the first 3 sts at right side of chart), place marker, beg again as shown, then work 16-st rep over next 80 sts, work next 6 sts as shown, place marker, then work rem 2 side sts.

Cont as est until Main Pattern is complete. Work Top Border Pattern (page 168) in same manner, working 40-st rep twice on center 80 sts of both front and back of pillow. Bind off.

FINISHING
Block pillow to finished measurements. Sew 2 rows of machine stitching along the 1st and 5th of the side sts at each side of pillow. Cut between machine stitching on both sides.

Main Pattern

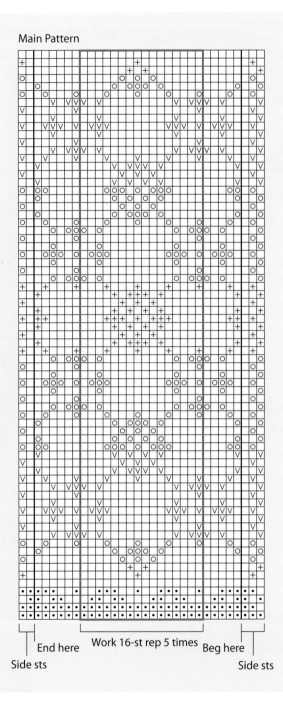

End here   Work 16-st rep 5 times   Beg here

Side sts   Side sts

blue grotto (MC)

● loden green (CC1)

＋ smoky rose (CC2)

◯ inca gold (CC3)

∨ linen (CC4)

repeat

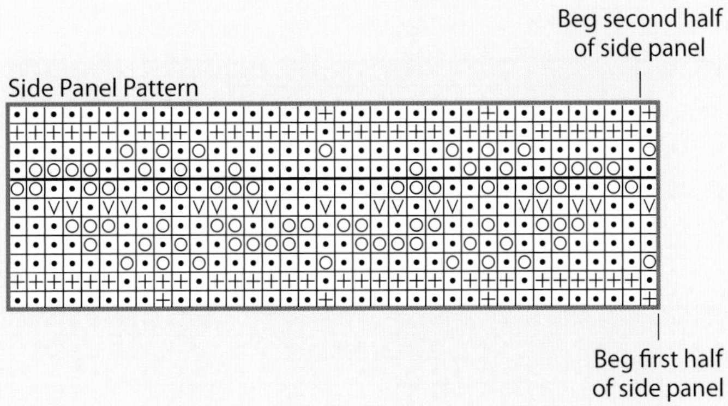

Side Panel Pattern

Beg second half
of side panel

Beg first half
of side panel

SIDE PANEL

With circ needle, CC1 and with RS facing, beg at lower-left corner and pick up 360 sts along bottom edge, right side, top, then down left side of one half of pillow (90 sts along each edge). Join and, working in the rnd, mark beg of rnd. Work first 6 rnds of Side Panel Pattern.

Cut yarns and slip last 8 sts from right needle back to left needle. Reattach CC1 and bind off 106 sts (the 90 sts along bottom, plus 8 sts on lower part of each side). Set aside.

With second circ needle, CC1, and with RS facing, beg at lower-right corner and pick up 360 sts along right side, top, left side, then bottom edges of rem half of pillow. Join and, working in the rnd, mark beg of rnd. Beg with last rnd of Side Panel Pattern and, reading from right to left, beg as shown on chart and work 5 rnds of pattern in reverse order (rnd 11 first, then rnd 10, then rnd 9 to rnd 7). Cut yarn and slip approx 96 sts from left needle to right needle so that left side of piece is at beg of new rnd, and adjust beg of rnd so patterns match when joining both halves.

JOINING

Hold both halves of pillow with RS tog, and bound-off edge of first half of pillow facing. Work three-needle bind-off using CC1 along sides and top of pillow. Bind off rem 106 sts of second half of pillow kwise on WS. Pin zipper into opening, then neatly sew to pillow. Insert pillow form.

Top Border Pattern

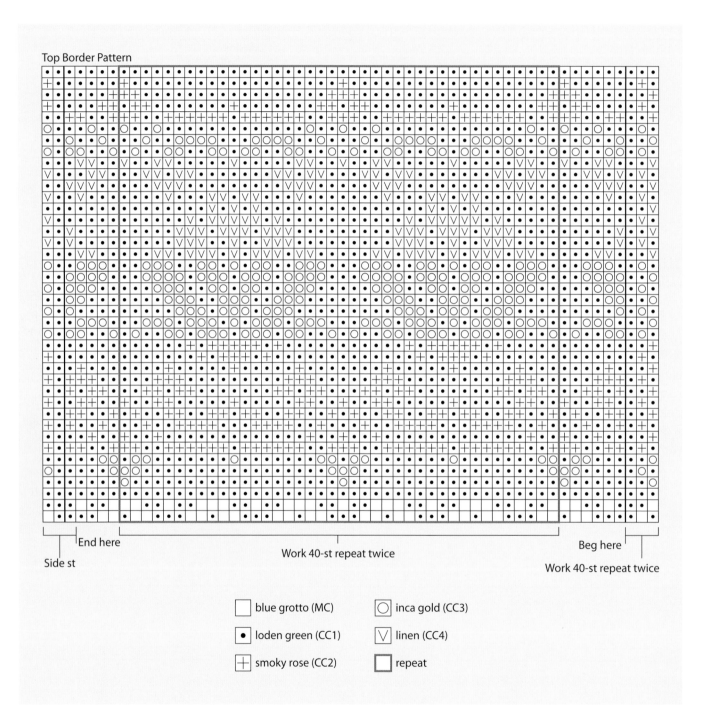

Side st

End here

Work 40-st repeat twice

Beg here

Work 40-st repeat twice

blue grotto (MC)   ⬡ inca gold (CC3)

● loden green (CC1)   ∨ linen (CC4)

+ smoky rose (CC2)   ⬜ repeat

Linen Jeans Purse

Inspired by Andean pattern motifs, this little purse is quick and easy to knit. Working from side to side is a great way to get a "vertical" pattern that's still worked in the round without ridiculously long floats on the wrong side of your work.

If you make this your first sew-and-cut finishing project, the initial terror of cutting will be over quickly and you'll see how easily these finishing techniques can be used on even small projects.

DIRECTIONS

PURSE

With MC, CO 90 sts. Join and, working in the rnd, make sure sts are not twisted. Mark beg of rnd.

Purl 1 rnd. Knit 5 rnds.

Following chart (page 173), work 29 rnds of Main Pattern.

With MC, knit 6 rnds, then purl 1 rnd. Bind off kwise.

Sew 2 rows of machine stitching on each side of rnd join, 2 sts out from beg and end of rnd.

Cut between machine stitching.

FLAP

Fold one cut edge to WS along line of sts 1 st in from machine stiching.

With MC and RS facing, beg with row above purl rnd at right edge and pick up and k32 sts along edge, through both layers. Working back and forth, beg with a WS row and work 3 rows of St st, making sure to slip first st of every row.

*Next row, slip 1 st, ssk, knit to last 3 sts, k2tog, end k1 st. Next row, slip 1 st, p2tog, purl to last 3 sts, skp, end p1 st. Work 1 row even. Next row, slip 1 st, p2tog, purl to last 3 sts, skp, end p1 st. Next row, slip 1 st, ssk, knit to last 3 sts, k2tog, end k1 st (24 sts). Work 1 row even.

Rep these 6 rows twice more, then first 2 dec rows once more (4 sts). Next row, slip first 2 sts individually kwise, k2tog, psso. Fasten off rem st.

Measurements
7" (18cm) wide × 9" (23cm) long

Yarn
Linen Jeans by Berroco (70% rayon/30% linen, 80 yd. [74m]/1³⁄₄ oz. [50g])
2 skeins, color #7405 New Khaki (MC)
1 skein, color #7428 Beet Root (CC)

Needles and Notions
Size 8 (5mm) circular needle 16" (40cm) long, or size needed to obtain gauge
Crochet hook size H/8 (5mm)
¹⁄₄ yd. (23cm) fabric for lining
Leather purse handle 42" (106.5cm)— Grayson E, brown, long, narrow
1 clasp—JHB International, #963 Classic Clasp
Stitch marker
Contrasting sewing thread
Sewing needle
Thread to match lining

Gauge
19 sts and 23 rnds over color work pattern = 4" (10cm)

➤ Take time to check your gauge.

Special Abbreviations
sc = single crochet
skp = slip 2 stitches, 1 at a time, kwise, slip both stitches together back to left needle, then purl together through back of loops.

new khaki (MC)

● beet root (CC)

repeat

Lay out purse to 7" × 18" (18cm × 45.5cm) long when measured between rows of machine stitching, with flap 4" (10cm) long. Steam lightly.

Fold rem cut edge to WS in same manner as first cut edge. Sew side seams using whip st.

EDGING

With CC and RS facing, attach yarn to top of bag at side seam with a slip st. Work 1 rnd of reverse sc along top edge, then along edge of flap. Fasten off.

LINING

Cut lining fabric to approx 7" × 18" (18cm × 45.5cm). Fold with RS tog and sew ³/₈" (1cm) seams along sides of lining. Fold approx ¹/₂" (1.5cm) along top edge to WS and steam lightly. Pin lining into purse with WS tog, and top of lining covering machine stitching and cut edges. Neatly sew lining to purse. If desired, sew handles and clasp to purse before sewing in lining. Before sewing in lining and to ensure a more stable place to sew purse handle and lower half of clasp to purse body, cut small pieces of lining fabric and baste to WS of purse where handles and lower half of clasp will be sewn to body of purse; if you baste the pieces of fabric without going through to the RS, you won't need to remove the basting once the purse is complete.

Sew handle to sides of purse. Sew clasp to flap and front of bag.

Yarn

Bonsai by Berroco (97% bamboo/3% nylon, 77 yd. [70m]/1¾ oz. [50g]) 12 skeins each #4164 Hotaka Gold

Seduce by Berroco (47% rayon/25% linen/17% silk/11% nylon, 100 yd. [100m]/1.41 oz. [40g]); 3 skeins color #4435 Chana Dal

Needles and Notions

1 U.S. size 6 (4mm) circular needle, or size needed to obtain gauge

1 U.S. size E/4 (3.5mm) crochet hook

Stitch markers

Contrasting sewing thread

Contrasting scrap yarn

Gauge

Before blocking, 21 sts and 31 rows over St st = 4" (10cm)

➤ Take time to check your gauge.

Crochet Abbreviations

ch = chain

dc = double crochet

hdc = half double crochet

sc = single crochet

slip st = slip stitch

tr = triple crochet

Crochet Stitches

Picot: Ch 3, work slip st in third ch from hook.

5-looped shell with chains: Work in ch-1 space [1 tr, ch1] 4 times, 1 tr.

6-looped shell with picots: Work in ch-1 space [2 tr, 1 picot] twice, 2 tr.

10-looped shell with picots: Work in ch-1 space, 2 tr, [1 picot, 3 tr in next ch-1 space] twice, 1 picot, 2 tr in next ch-1 space.

Bonsai Shawl

This shawl is a perfect example why you would want to use the sew-and-cut finishing method; the piece becomes rather heavy as it grows and if you were to work each side of the front separately there would be a lot of stretching going on, especially at the points where the fronts join the back at the neck bind off. The grafted seam of the facings disappear into the wrong side, making it almost as good looking as the right side.

I love crochet edgings and wanted to use that to finish off one of the projects in this book. If you don't crochet, consider an applied knitted lace, purchased lace or fringe, or simply leave the edge plain.

DIRECTIONS

BOTTOM EDGE

With Bonsai, cast on 7 sts using a provisional cast-on method. Working back and forth, beg with a WS row and work first 3 rows of Bottom Band chart (page 178), then rows 4–7 three more times and short row on rows indicated each time.

Beg 4-row rep and work until band measures approx 15" (38cm) from top of 3rd eyelet from beg (the last eyelet in short-rowed section at beg of edging). Work rows 4 – 7 four times and short row on rows indicated each time. Cut yarn.

SHAWL

With RS facing, remove provisional CO and slip resulting sts to spare needle. Work first 5 sts of Right Side chart, p2tog, yo, place marker, pick up 70 sts along edge of bottom band (pick up each st through one loop along edge, not both loops), place marker, yo, p2tog, work last 5 sts of Left Side chart—84 sts. Cont back and forth, and work side charts at each side, with St st over rem sts until there are 204 sts, ending with a WS row. Shawl should measure approx 18" (45.5cm) from bottom edge.

NECK OPENING

Next row (RS), work Right Side Pattern, k2tog, k81 sts, bind off the next 24 sts for neck opening, k81 sts, ssk, work Left Side Pattern. Next row, CO 4 cutting sts over bound off sts of previous row.

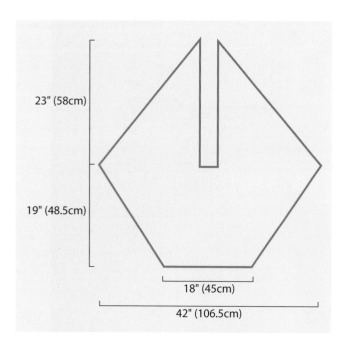

23" (58cm)

19" (48.5cm)

18" (45cm)

42" (106.5cm)

Next row, cont pattern and, **at the same time,** shape front edges in this manner: on **RS rows,** work Right Side Pattern, k2tog, knit to 2 sts before Left Side Pattern, ssk, then work Left Side Pattern—2 sts dec. Work WS rows even. Rep these 2 rows until all sts have been dec out of work on both sides of cutting sts. Bind off.

FINISHING

Sew 2 rows of machine stitching along each side of cutting sts for front opening.

OUTER EDGING

With Seduce, crochet hook and with RS facing, work 653 sc along outer edges of shawl (first row of chart), making sure to work 2 sc in the 2 or 3 sts at each corner. Work rem 3 rows of chart, working 6 tr in each corner for row 3 and 3 tr groups in each corner on row 4. Fasten off.

FRONT FACINGS

Cut between the machine stitching.

With circ needle, Bonsai and with RS facing, beg at bottom of cut edge on right side of front opening and pick up and k117 sts along right front, 27 sts along neck, then 117 sts along left front edges—261 sts. Working back and forth, beg with a WS row. K116 for fold line, k2tog, bind off next 25 kwise, k2tog, then knit to end of row for fold line—117 sts rem on each side of front. Working each side of front separately, work 6 rows of St st. Trim cut edge of any loose ends. Turn facing toward shawl, covering cut edge, then graft sts to WS using Kitchener st.

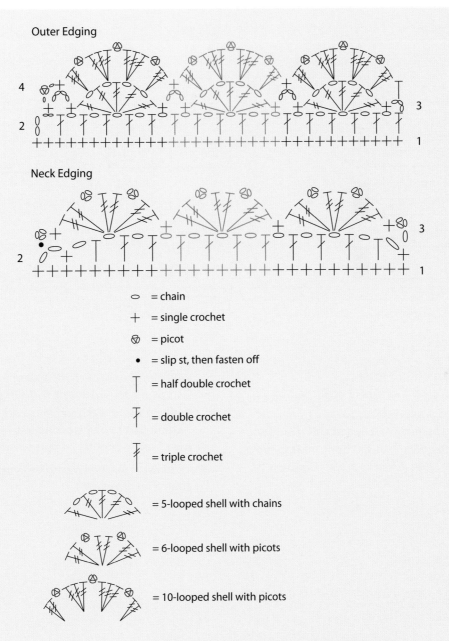

Outer Edging

Neck Edging

○ = chain

+ = single crochet

⊗ = picot

• = slip st, then fasten off

T = half double crochet

↑ = double crochet

↑ = triple crochet

= 5-looped shell with chains

= 6-looped shell with picots

= 10-looped shell with picots

Note: Stitches marked in purple denote pattern repeat

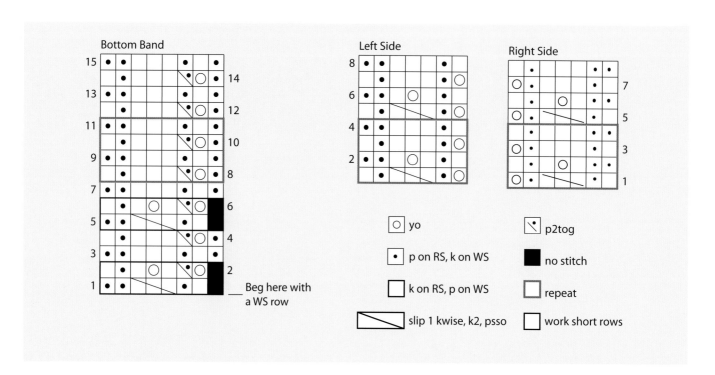

FRONT AND NECK EDGING

With Seduce, crochet hook and with RS facing, beg at side edge of row 2 along outer edging on right front and work 261 sc along opening and neck edges to side edge of row 2 along outer edging on left front, making sure to work through purl ridge in fold lines and bound-off sts.

Work rem 2 rows of chart, ending row 2 by working last 2 sts over edges of rows 3 and 4 of outer edging and skipping 2 sts at each corner of neck instead of skipping 1 st. End last row by working last 2 sts over edges of rows 3 and 4 of outer edging on other side. Fasten off.

Block shawl to finished measurements, pinning crochet edging by picots only.

Knitting Abbreviations

ABBREVIATIONS	MEANING
approx	approximately
beg	begin, beginning
CC	contrast color
circ	circular
cn	cable needle
CO	cast on
cont	continue, continuing
dec	decrease, decreasing
dpn(s)	double pointed needle(s)
est	establish, established
inc	increase, increasing
k	knit
k4tog	knit 4 stitches together (3 stitches decreased)
k2tog	knit 2 stitches together (1 stitch decreased)
kwise	knit-wise, as if to knit
MC	main color
p	purl
p-loop	purl loop
p2tog	purl 2 stitches together (1 stitch decreased)

ABBREVIATIONS	MEANING
psso	pass slipped stitch (or stitches) over
pwise	purl-wise, as if to purl
rem	remain(s), remaining, remainder
rnd(s)	round(s)
RS	right side(s)
ssk	slip, slip, knit or slip 2 stitches knit-wise, 1 at a time, insert left needle through front of both stitches and knit through the back of the loops (1 stitch decreased)
st(s)	stitch(es)
St st	stockinette stitch
tbl	through the back of the loop(s)
tog	together
WS	wrong side(s)
yo	yarn over

BIBLIOGRAPHY

Allen, Pam. *Knitting for Dummies*. Indianapolis, Indiana: Wiley Publishing, 2002.

Compton, Rae. *The Complete Book of Traditional Knitting*. New York: Charles Scribner's Sons, 1984.

Dahlin, Judith B. *Knitting Norwegian Sweaters*. St. Paul, Minnesota: Dos Tejedoras, 1994.

Dale Yarn Company. *Knit Your Own Norwegian Sweaters*. New York: Dover Publications, 1974.

Editors of Vogue Knitting. *Vogue Knitting: Ultimate Knitting Book*. New York: Sixth&Spring Books, 2002.

Feitelson, Ann. *The Art of Fair Isle Knitting: History, Technique, Color & Patterns*. Loveland, Colorado: Interweave Press, 1996.

Finseth, Mararetha, ed. *Norsk Strikkedesign*. Petaluma, California; Unicorn Books and Crafts, 2002.

Gibson-Roberts, Priscilla A; and Robson, Deborah. *Knitting in the Old Way: Designs & Techniques from Ethnic Sweaters*. Fort Collins, Colorado: Nomad Press, 2004.

Hisdal, Solveig. *Poetry in Stitches: Clothes You can Knit*. Oslo, Norway: N. W. Damm & Søn, 2000.

Knitting Around the World. Threads. Newtown, Connecticut: Taunton Press, 1993.

Kolstad, Lisa; and Takle, Tone. *More Sweaters: A Riot of Color, Pattern, and Form*. Loveland, Colorado: Interweave Press, 1994.

—*Small Sweaters: Colorful Knits for Kids*. Loveland, Colorado: Interweave Press, 1996.

—*Sweaters: 28 Contemporary Designs in the Norwegian Tradition*. Loveland, Colorado: Interweave Press, 1992.

Lewandowski, Marica. *Andean Folk Knits*. New York: Lark Books, 2005.

Lind, Vibeke. *Knitting in the Nordic Tradition*. Asheville, North Carolina: Lark Books, 1984.

McGregor, Sheila. *The Complete Book of Traditional Fair Isle Knitting*. New York: Charles Scribner's Sons, 1981.

—*Traditional Scandinavian Knitting*. Mineola, New York: Dover Publications, 2004.

Morgan, Gwyn. *Traditional Knitting Patterns of Ireland, Scotland and England*. New York: St. Martin's Press, 1981.

Pagoldh, Susanne. *Nordic Knitting*. Loveland, Colorado: Interweave Press, 1991.

Pearl-McPhee, Stephanie. *Knitting Rules!* North Adams, Massachusetts: Storey Publishing, 2006.

Starmore, Alice. *Alice Starmore's Book of Fair Isle Knitting*. Newtown, Connecticut: Taunton Press. 1988.

—*Fair Isle Without Fear* (video tape). New York: Publisher's Video, 1994.

Sundbø, Annemor. *Setesdal Sweaters: The History of the Norwegian Lice Pattern*. Kristiansand, Norway: Torridal Tweed, 2001.

Swansen, Meg. *Cardigan Details* (videotape). Pittsville, Wisconsin: Schoolhouse Press, 1994.

Zimmermann, Elizabeth. *Knitting Without Tears*. New York: Simon & Schuster, 1971.

Resources

Therese Chynoweth teaches classes and workshops on the topics covered in this book. For information on where she is teaching, or how to schedule a workshop, please contact her at inkandwool@yahoo.com and include "workshops" in the subject line. For a list of knitting publications and information on blocking, go to www.wiley.com/go/norwegiansweatertechniques.

Yarns

Be Sweet
1315 Bridgeway
Sausalito, CA 94965
www.besweetproducts.com

Berroco, Inc.
14 Elmdale Rd.
P. O. Box 367
Uxbridge, MA 01569
www.berroco.com

Blue Sky Alpacas Inc.
P. O. Box 88
Cedar, MN 55011
www.blueskyalpacas.com

Classic Elite Yarns
122 Western Ave.
Lowell, MA 01851
www.classiceliteyarns.com

Dale of Norway, Inc.
4750 Shelburne Rd., Suite 20
Shelburne, VT 05482
www.daleofnorway.com

Knit One, Crochet Too, Inc.
91 Tandberg Trail, Unit #6
Windham, ME 04602
www.knitonecrochettoo.com

Lorna's Laces
4229 N. Honore St.
Chicago, IL 60613
www.lornaslaces.net

Plymouth Yarn
500 Lafayette St.
Bristol, PA 19007
www.plymouthyarn.com

SWTC, Inc.
918 S. Park Lane, Suite 102
Tempe, AZ 85281
www.soysilk.com

Tahki Stacy Charles
7030 80th St.
Ridgewood, NY 11385
www.tahkistacycharles.com

Universal Yarn
284 Ann St.
Concord, NC 28025
www.universalyarn.com

Vermont Organic Fiber Co.
52 Seymour St., Suite 8
Middlebury, VT 05753
www.o-wool.com
O-Wool yarns and distributors for Danforth Pewter buttons

Westminster Fibers, Inc.
8 Ledge Dr.
Greer, SC 29650
www.westminsterfibers.com
Distributors for Rowan and Nashua Handknits yarns

Buttons and accessories

Annie Adams Adornments Inc.
810 Elmwood Ave.
Buffalo, NY 14222
www.annieadams.com

JHB International, Inc.
1955 S. Quince St.
Denver, CO 80231
www.buttons.com

Moving Mud
1178 Senor Rd.
Warren, VT 05674
www.movingmud.com

Muench Yarns, Inc.
1323 Scott St.
Petaluma, CA 94954
www.muenchyarns.com
Distributors for Grayson E leather purse handles

Index